SyberVision

Muscle Memory Programming for Every Sport

by Steven DeVore and Greggory R. DeVore, MD
with Mike Michaelson

Delta Lithograph Co.
14731 California St.
Van Nuys, CA 91411-3195

Library of Congress Cataloging in Publication Data

DeVore, Steven.
SyberVision, muscle memory programming for every sport.

1. Physical education and training. 2. Muscles.
I. DeVore, Greggory R. II. Michaelson, Mike, 1934-
III. Title.
GV711.5.D48   613.7'1   81-3886
ISBN 0-914090-98-4   AACR2

First edition
Fourth printing

ISBN cl 0-0914090-98-4
     pa 0-914091-01-8

Cover Design by Steve McKinley

Printed by Delta Lithograph Co., 14731 Califa St.,
Van Nuys, CA 91411-3195

This book is dedicated to Helen Kuykendall DeVore, our mother, whose innate wisdom in healing a crippled child will cause a profound revolution in human performance training.

ACKNOWLEDGEMENTS

We would like gratefully to acknowledge the following individuals who have voluntarily contributed time and effort to the development of SyberVision.

Wesley DeVore, Helen DeVore, Jim DeVore, Ollie B. DeVore, Stan Clark, Andy Been, Gonzalo Rodriguez, Les Burns, Ron Yates, Jan Hutchins, Pete Liebengood, Stephanie Salter, Mitchell Page, Howard Jamison, Dick Gould, Frank Brennan, Rick Schavone, Jim and Shokoo Ghosseiri, Craig Fisher, Sarah Rabinovicci, The 1980 Stanford Men's and Women's Tennis Team, Dick Kuchen, Doug True, Regan Jones, Ron Jones, Michael Sparks, Dan Danielson, Mary Anne Strom, Mike Strom, William Mathews Brooks, Don Rasmussen, Don Murphy, Darrly Carr, Susan Silverberg, Houshang Shabestari, Bong Mo, Greg Hing, Turk Schonert, Ken Margerum, Lisa Gessini, Albert Nebeker, and a score of special people who have dedicated their time and efforts to the SyberVision Program.

We would also like to acknowledge the voluntary contribution of Brian Hennessy, Researcher at Stanford University, whose knowledge and intensity have contributed greatly to the SyberVision Program.

A special acknowledgement to our wives and children for their sacrifice, effort and understanding: Kathy, Tara, Steven and Julie DeVore and Dorothy, Greggory, Trevor, and Nathan DeVore.

And, finally, a heartfelt acknowledgement to Nasser Hamedani, whose sacrifice, hard work, faith and humor have been the driving force behind the SyberVision program, and to his wife Andrea and their family: Mamma Jon, Sholeh, Daniel, Soraiya and Roaya, who have also borne the burden of its development.

Contents

1

Introduction: The Five Percent Factor

If you can imagine a powerful mental and physical sports training program that . . .

• would allow you to achieve in one hour what you normally would accomplish in 10 to 20 hours of physical practice under perfect conditions;

• is more advanced and effective than the most sophisticated sports training technology developed by the Soviet Union and East Germany;

• would advance your skill level two years in only three months of training;

• has been heralded by internationally respected doctors, psychologists, physiologists, coaches, trainers and athletes as "revolutionary";

• will take an athlete at the five percent consistency level (able to perform a desirable motion or stroke only five out of 100 attempts) and enable him or her to perform at the 50 to 80 percent consistency level—no matter what the age or sport activity

. . . if you can imagine all of this, then you can begin to grasp the staggering potential of SyberVision.

There's no need to use your imagination, because Syber-Vision exists. It is a proven system, a system that works. And it is totally accessible to any weekend athlete who has ever struggled for consistency at just about any sport, because the nucleus of success already lies within you, buried within the recesses and convolutions of your brain. The tissues of your brain right now contain electronic codes or "blueprints" of those precise, fundamentally sound movements that you already have performed in your sporadic moments of excellence in play and competition.

If you have ever served the tennis ball correctly or driven the golf ball solidly and straight, then your brain and muscles already know how to perform the action. If you have bowled the perfect strike, thrown the perfect swish through the basketball hoop, the memory of that action is etched indelibly in your brain. If you have thrown the perfect pitch, hit the perfect line drive or skied the perfect run, then it is within your ability to do it over and over again, unerringly and consistently. And it is consistency that spells the difference between the winning and losing athlete—consistency that determines whether the weekend athlete derives personal satisfaction or embarrassing frustration from his or her sport.

Consistency. That is the key to improving your sports performance. No matter whether you are a pro, a talented amateur or a weekend hacker, the powerful SyberVision system of muscle-memory programming will allow you to stimulate, activate, consistently recall and execute that stored memory for an amazingly high level of performance in play and competition—no matter what your sport.

Until the publication of this book, the powerful SyberVision formula for muscle memory programming has been available only to those professional or serious amateur athletes who could afford to pay the thousands of dollars for the program or to university-level elite athletes who have engaged in Syber-Vision research programs. Now, after years of research, development and testing, the complete SyberVision formula and training system is being made available to the public, to the aspiring athlete who demands more of himself or herself than he or she now is achieving.

SyberVision is not a teaching program that starts off by dictatorially telling you to "forget everything you ever learned" about your sport. On the contrary, through SyberVision techniques you will learn how to reinforce all of the sound fundamentals you have "learned" (but not mastered) through years of practice and play. SyberVision is a proven, effective system for programming and unleashing your reservoir of positively stored muscle memory. It has enabled professional, collegiate and world-class athletes to maximize their performances . . . with startling results. Now it is available to you, in an easy-to-follow, step-by-step format.

First, SyberVision will teach you a discipline to make your muscles respond fluidly and automatically to the intent of your mind through a process called Syber-Relaxation.

Second, you will learn a powerful technique of developing performance-enhancing concentration—Syber-Concentration. This is a grooved and single-minded channel of thought through which the electronically encoded "blueprints" of desirable movement can travel to activate relaxed and primed muscle tissue for precise, coordinated movement.

Third, you'll learn the formula for Syber-Coding muscle memory, using televised sports programs to stimulate and bring to the surface for easy access the memory of fundamental skills already stored in your brain. Instead of viewing sports as a passive spectator, you'll find yourself using your home screen as a 21st century laboratory of learning, one that can help you measurably improve your own performance at your favorite sport.

The fourth SyberVision skill you will master is a potent technique for activating your stored muscle memory for the consistent execution of skills in practice and play. And once you begin to enjoy an increased level of consistency, you will learn how to retain, build and expand your consistency into a deep reservoir of muscle memory. This will lead to the habitual execution of desirable skills. You won't have to think about how to do it—it will be automatic.

Golf pros develop muscle memory by spending endless hours, day after day, week after week, on the practice tee. Scientific research has shown that it takes up to 400 hours of consistent, repetitious practice for a physical motion to become automatic—a conditioned "habit" reflex. That is up to 400 hours— or about 10 work weeks!—of consistently practicing the right action.

In the pressure cooker of competition for high stakes, this programmed mastery of the fundamentals has a big pay-off. It allows the professional to put his or her playing skills on "automatic pilot" and concentrate on the dynamics of a winning strategy rather than worrying about whether or not the strokes will be "there."

Obviously, the weekend athlete is unable to devote these long hours of practice to make the fundamentals of a sport the kind of conditioned habit that produces consistent near-flawless performances. The few precious free hours available to the weekend athlete should be spent in enjoyment of the sport rather than in the frustrations associated with sporadic performance. Yet, for a vast majority of weekend athletes, even a modest level of performance excellence is a fleeting and elusive dream. SyberVision will show you how to develop the same quality and depth of muscle memory that the pros work so hard to develop and retain—the kind of reflexive know-how that sends drives splitting the center of the fairway and guides a bowling ball into the pocket frame after frame. And it will help you to acquire those reflexes in about 90 percent less time than you now spend in your sports training.

For every three months you practice your sport using the SyberVision system, your skill and consistency level will progress at least two years ahead of where you otherwise would be!

As an athlete struggling for consistency in your sport, you have had those rare and rapturous moments when everything you did seemed to be grooved. Your body and mind seemed to work together in harmony. You felt relaxed, intensively concentrated and aggressive. Your movement was fluid and cat-like— your every move seemed to be an expression of pure instinct. You were invincible!

Such an experience you will never forget. Every time you compete you try to recapture it. You know deep down inside that because you have experienced "greatness" before, it should be within your inherent potential to do it again. But such a superb performance seems to be left to the mercy of the gods—an occurrence whose frequency you can neither predict nor control.

The SyberVision system of muscle-memory programming allows you to understand the dynamics behind consistent performance and then enables you to apply those principles to the rapid and continual improvement of your performance. It is based on the assumption that if you can perform the fundamentals of your sport correctly a minimum of five times out of 100 attempts, then it is possible for a high level of consistent performance to become a reality for you.

Every time you practice your sport you are working from previously stored muscle memory. If you can produce a desirable motion at the five percent level of consistency, then a muscle memory blueprint, or an electronically encoded pattern of that movement, is dispersed throughout memory in your brain. SyberVision gives you the necessary tools to stimulate, activate, recall, perform and store that memory for consistent, fluid movement. It will help you develop the high quality motions, strokes and movements that will put you at the top of your playing potential.

Probably, you have already experienced the SyberVision Phenomenon. After being a spectator at a tennis match, golf tournament or basketball game or after watching a great performance of your favorite sport on television, you may have gone out to play later that day or the following morning and found yourself playing a great game without ever knowing why.

You played as if you had momentarily assimilated the timing, rhythm and fine-tuned control of those you so intently watched. On the tennis court your strokes were grooved. Your shots went where you wanted them to go, at the desired velocity and angle. As a golfer, you suddenly found that your swing was relaxed and controlled, as a bowler you found yourself blocking in more strikes on the score sheet.

Without consciously trying to imitate the style and mechanics of the pros you watched hours before, you found yourself playing as if you were a mental and physical recreation of those who inspired your play.

Unfortunately, after a few short but memorable playing moments, the groove effect wears off. Your game slips back to its original level of consistent inconsistency. Thereafter, every time you try to recall or capture the feeling of the relaxed, concentrated and fluid movement associated with the phenomenon, the mental blueprint to which it was attached seems to bury itself deeper into the recesses of memory. In an attempt to physically stimulate and activate that memory, you become so tense and frustrated that the game you want to play for pleasure becomes a laborious task.

While the groove effect lasted, you were experiencing the SyberVision Phenomenon. You had briefly and gloriously stepped outside of yourself, playing off the five percent or so of fundamentally sound memory that was stimulated by the vision, sound, emotion and perceived "touch" sensations generated by the source of the feedback you were absorbing.

When the groove effect slipped away, you were working counter to the principles and laws which govern this phenomenon. Instead of using your head to your ultimate advantage, you were unmercifully beating it against the backboard wall.

The SyberVision discipline of muscle-memory programming outlined in this book will teach you to understand and control the physical and mental laws that govern this phenomenon. It will enable you to apply this knowledge immediately to dramatically improve your sports performance.

The techniques detailed in this book are the result of modern advances in the sciences of medicine, psychology and electronics. SyberVision is the product of the most dramatic and profound theories and research within these sciences.

The SyberVision training system was not the result of an instant inspiration. It evolved from the work of two brothers: Dr. Greggory DeVore, a 34-year-old physician at the Yale University School of Medicine, and his brother, Steven DeVore, a 29-year-old educational sports psychologist and president of Professional Development Associates, Inc.—a firm specializing in the training of professional and world-class athletes.

The rationale behind SyberVision began when Steven DeVore was three years old. Stricken with crippling polio, he was told that he never would walk again. Through a stringent discipline of physical and mental exercise (later researched, refined and validated as a germane part of the SyberVision system of muscle-memory programming) Steven "miraculously" regained the use of his muscles, relearned the mechanics of

Steve DeVore at age 3, sparring with World Heavyweight Boxing Champion Max Baer in Children's Hospital, Oakland, California.

walking and went on to excel at competitive athletics.

While in college, Steven had a profound experience with the SyberVision Phenomenon that seemed to provide one of the missing links to the ultimate development of the SyberVision program. One wintery Saturday afternoon, Steven, an undergraduate student at Brigham Young University, was holed up in his living room reading and idly watching television. His attention drifted from his studying to the professional bowlers on television who were racking up strike after strike. Himself an occasional bowler—an unspectacular 163 his best game ever—Steven began speculating as to whether he could put that televised bowling program to practical use. He wondered whether it could serve as a source of feedback to stimulate the best of his then-dormant bowling muscle memory. He decided to try.

Drawing on the same muscle relaxation, concentration and memory activation he mastered as a child in his successful battle against polio, Steven focused his complete attention upon the action on the television screen. He locked himself into a high level of concentration, blocking out everything else, allowing the actions of the professional bowlers scattering the pins to etch themselves into his memory.

Afterward he played this program back in his mind. Then he devised for himself a color cue. This would serve as a catalyst to set in motion his mentally-stored video tape. Then he and a friend headed for a neighboring bowling center to test his theory.

The results of that experiment were remarkable. In his first game, Steven bowled nine straight strikes. In his second game, he rolled eight strikes. Then the phenomenon began to gradually diminish until he was back to his normal level of performance. Although he couldn't maintain the high level of consistency, Steven DeVore knew he had discovered a phenomenon that had universal applications that should be further researched and tested.

To gain a further understanding of what had happened, and with the goal of controlling the resulting high level of performance for continued consistency, Steven and Greggory DeVore during the following years collaborated in their research efforts, pooling their knowledge and experience to formulate the basic principles which now underlie the SyberVision system.

To test the effectiveness of the newly developed theory and program, Steven approached California State University at Hayward varsity tennis coach, Dr. Stan Clark, and proposed an experiment. "Give me some of your lowest ranking tennis players, individuals who you feel could never possibly break into your starting line-up under normal conditions and let's see what effect, if any, the program would have on their competitive performance." Subsequently, two of the lowest ranking players on Clark's squad, Andy Been and Gonzalo Rodriguez, volunteered for the program. The results made international news.

In only two weeks after starting the SyberVision program, recalls Clark, "both Been and Rodriguez miraculously broke into the team's starting line-up." Been, a freshman, completed the entire tennis season with only one defeat while Rodriguez, a senior, went undefeated in league play. Rodriquez earned the right to compete in the NCAA II national single's championships where he barely was defeated by the national clay court champion.

Commented Dr. Clark: "In all of my years of coaching I have never seen such rapid progress in athletes before."

Other SyberVision success stories include the 1977 *Sporting News* Rookie of the Year Mitchell Page of the Oakland A's. In mid-season 1979, when Page was in a horrendous batting slump, hitting in the low .200s, he decided to go through the SyberVision program. During the six weeks Page was involved in the program he hit an impressive .348. The following year during spring training he hit confidently for a .444 average. The evening of one memorable SyberVision session, Page hit two towering home runs. The last time he had accomplished that feat was in 1977 during his rookie year against the Boston Red Sox in Fenway Park. Incredibly, the televised feedback Page was using as his memory activation source was a video tape of those two home runs in Boston. Page's second home run that evening in Oakland was one of the longest balls ever hit in the Oakland-Alameda County Coliseum. During the last 25 games of the season Page hit an unbelievable 12 home runs—which he attributed to the SyberVision system of muscle memory programming. The story of Mitchell Page and SyberVision was featured on ABC television's "That's Incredible" in March, 1981.

Other SyberVision successes include the 1980 Stanford University men's tennis team. Using the SyberVision system, Stanford captured the 1980 NCAA National Championship. Dick Gould, Stanford tennis coach, believes that the SyberVision program was the critical factor in his 1980 success:

"In my opinion, the SyberVision discipline helped my players to play consistently under the intense pressure of competition. It allowed them to relax, concentrate and to draw from the rich reservoir of SyberVision-stimulated muscle memory. Instead of giving my players the traditional pep talks I just had them key into the SyberVision memory activation formula and then let the rest happen naturally."

In summary, Gould noted: "I think the SyberVision program is powerful and has the potential to help create a superior athlete."

It made a believer out of Doug True, a graduate of the University of California Berkeley and a member of the 1979 Cal basketball team. He used the SyberVision system to program himself for a career high game of 30 points. True raised his shooting percentage to such a level that he was drafted by the Phoenix Suns of the NBA and, according to the Sun coach, would have made the team if he had not decided on a career in engineering rather than basketball.

Bowling professional Marshall Holman, at age 25 one of only three bowlers to top $100,000 in annual earnings on the pro circuit, also is a SyberVision alumnus. "It's a powerful thing," says Holman. "The mental impact is real strong. It allows me to key into past success to establish success in key situations."

The list of SyberVision success stories is nearly endless. The key fact to keep in mind—the bottom line for anyone struggling for consistency in any sport—is that the SyberVision system of muscle programming works. And it will work for you.

SyberVision gives you 21st Century training systems NOW. In a full-page feature in the editorial section, *The Denver Post* heralded SyberVision as "a secret weapon technology that was transforming sports" and "the most powerfully effective system of sports training in the world—even more advanced than any procedures the Soviet countries now utilize."

Dr. A. Craig Fisher, chairman of graduate physical education programs at Ithaca College in New York and the author of the definitive college textbook, *The Psychology of Sport,* believes that SyberVision training will eventually revolutionize sports training. "To remain competitive over the Russians in international Olympic-type competition," notes Dr. Fisher, "our athletes will have to adopt a SyberVision-type training model. Every major college team will have to incorporate such sophisticated and powerful techniques if it desires to maintain a winning posture. The future of sports training is probably SyberVision."

Dr. Gregory Raiport, former sports psychologist for USSR

Olympic training, strongly agrees. Of SyberVision he says, "At last the West has come up with a sports training system that seems to be superior to the most advanced Soviet training technology."

Dr. Richard Schavone, Stanford University sports psychologist and an Olympic coach, states: "SyberVision is one of the most concrete, theoretically sound, strongest programs of sport performance development and improvement in existence today."

Dr. Sarah Jaque, a medical physicist and world renowned researcher in human physiology at the Hebrew University in Jerusalem believes that SyberVision has the potential for revolutionizing human performance training. "I know for a certainty," she says, "that any individuals trained in Syber-Vision skills will have a sharper mental discipline, refined performance skills and a quicker reaction time with which to respond to their sport. SyberVision, I feel, will become the most powerful discipline in maximizing human performance."

Now the SyberVision techniques that have catapulted hundreds of athletes to personal success in their sports and that have commanded a following of respected scientists and sports experts are available to readers of this book.

SyberVision can be applied to any sport or any physical activity. All you need is the simple proficiency to execute the desirable and fundamental movements of your sport at the five percent level. This book will show you how to increase your current consistency factor to more than 50 percent.

If you are not already a pro, SyberVision cannot promise to make you one. But it can help you perform like a pro more consistently than you ever thought possible.

The emotional experience of observing his brother's recovery inspired Gregg DeVore to pursue a career in medicine and in college and graduate school impelled Steven to research the dynamics of his personal conquest.

2

Are You a Natural Athlete?

Picture yourself in an English pub, cosy, warm and friendly. The inevitable dart game is in progress and you are invited to play. You step up to the foul line, take the flighted metal shaft in your hand, raise it to eye level, sight it with the target, and let fly. Whether the dart travels straight and true into the bull's eye, evoking an enthusiastic "Well done," from your British friends, or whether it misses the target entirely (evoking a polite "Nice try,") largely is a matter of hand-eye coordination (discounting, of course, the effects of British hospitality).

All of us have heard of an athlete—even a beginning athlete —described as "a natural" or as being "gifted." Maybe someone has even made such a comment about you—perhaps when you hit the bull's eye the very first time you threw a dart! Usually, this "naturalness" has nothing to do with acquired skills at a particular sport. It refers to a high degree of co-ordination that "gifted" person has between the eye and the body.

Just about all of the sports we play put a premium on this coordination between the eye and the body. In games such as golf, tennis, bowling and basketball, where we are aiming at a

SyberVision test for eye dominance

target, hand-eye coordination is particularly important. Even in a "non-target" sport such as skiing, this alignment between eye and body is crucial as a skier maneuvers to negotiate the twists and curves of the slope.

This coordination may come naturally to you, or you may have to work on it. Either way, the SyberVision program will help you increase your ability to align eye and body as you work toward greater consistency at your favorite sport.

Most of us have a dominant side of the body. We are right- or left-handed, we have a dominant right or left leg and foot. Most of us usually have one dominant eye that we rely on when we are aligning with a target—for example, the eye that remains open when we sight along the barrel of a rifle.

Those so-called natural athletes who are easily able to align eye and body to a target—a tennis ball, a golf ball, bowling pins—usually find that their dominant side of the body and their dominant eye coincide. They are purely **right-side dominant** or **left-side dominant**. Such athletes find that the fundamentals of the sport are easily learned and afterwards executed with a high degree of performance consistency.

Those who struggle to hit a target—those who have greater difficulty in hitting that bull's eye—usually will turn out to be **cross-dominant**. This means that the dominant eye and the dominant side of the body are opposite. These athletes will experience extreme fluctuations in consistency; one day everything will be "all together," the next day everything falls apart.

To find out whether you have natural eye-and-body co-ordination (right-side dominant or left-side dominant) or whether you are cross-dominant, try the following test.

TEST FOR DOMINANCE

Note: Instructions for the following test are for right-handed persons. If you are left-handed, simply reverse the procedure.

1. Extend your right arm straight out in front of your body so that your hand is aligned with the tip of your nose.

2. Raise the index finger so that it is perpendicular to the ground—or hold a pen, pencil or similar object so that it is perpendicular to the ground.

3. With both eyes open, align your raised index finger or held object with some fixed object at head height about 10 feet distant, e.g. the knob of a cabinet, a wall-mounted thermostat.

4. Close first the right eye, then open the right eye, then close the left eye—successively sighting your target object with the open eye.

Conclusions

1. If, when you closed your left eye and sighted with the right eye, your index finger or held object remained on target, you are right-eye dominant. Since you are right-handed, your eye-and-body coordination are identical. You will have noticed that when you closed your right eye and sighted with your left eye, your target object appeared to jump off to the right.

2. If the target object appeared to jump when you sighted with your right eye and to remain steady when you used your left eye for sighting, you are cross-dominant—with a dominant right body and a dominant left eye.

As we have noted, persons who are cross-dominant usually lack that natural ability to align with a target that characterizes athletes who are strictly right- or left-dominant. At the bowling lanes or on the golf course they find it necessary to make adjustments to compensate for this imbalance.

Athletes who take the Dominance Test at the SyberVision Training Center in California and who are shown to be cross-dominant undergo a simple corrective program. It is one that readers of this book can easily follow at home.

To accustom the lazy eye to take up more of the workload (if you are cross-dominant), we recommend training with an eye patch. Worn over the dominant eye during practice—and even for an hour or two each day around the home—this places the burden of alignment onto the other eye and allows you to build a more natural eye-body coordination.

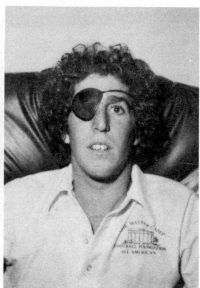

Ken Margerum, former Stanford University wide receiver, wearing an eye patch to correct cross-dominance.

HAND-EYE-COORDINATION EXERCISES

As we have noted, most of the sports we play require a high degree of hand-eye coordination—even such "non-target" sports as skiing. The following series of exercises is designed to help you develop this coordination. Spend about 30 minutes working at each exercise—not to any particular schedule, simply when you have some spare time. You'll probably find that they are fun, as well as helpful to your game.

SyberJacks

This is a variation of the children's game which uses a rubber ball and five small metal objects—jacks—each with six small arms. The object is to toss the ball in the air and pick up the

SyberVision eye-hand coordination exercises: SyberStraws

jacks, first one, then two at a time, and so on, before the ball comes down. In our version, you use an eye patch, as follows:
1. Cover right eye and use right hand.
2. Switch to left hand with right eye still covered.
3. Cover left eye and use left hand.
4. Switch to right hand with left eye still covered.
5. Without patch, use right hand (as in regular jacks).
6. Repeat with left hand.

SyberStraws

For this exercise you need a partner. Equipment is a drinking straw and a thin, plastic stick that will slide into the straw (sticks used in the "pick-up sticks" game are ideal). The object is to have your partner point the straw toward you as you attempt to thread your stick in and out of the tube. In addition to promoting hand-eye coordination, this exercise enhances depth perception. Alternate eye patch and use of hands as in the previous exercise.

SyberChopsticks

If you are a dyed-in-the-wool flatware person who insists on receiving a fork in a Chinese restaurant, you may want to skip this one. It calls for using chopsticks to pick an object up from a flat surface. Start out with a manageable object, such as a playing dice, and graduate to something more difficult, such as a coin. This exercise helps fine-tune your motor movement. Alternate eye patch and use of hands as in previous exercises— and then try it with your eyes closed.

SyberPitchback

All you need for this exercise is a ball and a wall (or you could use a trampoline or a pitchback device). In addition to coordination, this exercise helps improve depth perception and reaction time. Simply play one-handed catch with yourself,

SyberVision eye-hand coordination exercises: SyberAim

starting slowly and gradually increasing the speed. Alternate eye patch and use of hands as in previous exercises.

SyberDarts

You won't need the English pub we talked about earlier in this chapter but you will need dartboard and darts. Alternating eye patch and hands as in previous exercises, aim your dart at the bull's eye from the standard throwing distance of eight feet. This exercise is a good aid to alignment (putters take note).

Putting

Golfers can also put the eye patch to good use as they practice on the putting green. Alternate the patch between your left and right eye and then discard it as you gradually increase your distance from the hole, beginning at three feet and working out to 20 feet.

SyberAim

For this exercise, you are a bombardier with a bunch of pencils as your missiles and a cookie or mayonnaise jar as your target. Stand on a chair, take aim and let fly. This exercise promotes hand-eye coordination and alignment. Alternate eye patch and use of hands as in earlier exercises. (Explain to boss that you are: a. testing a new theory of time and motion; b. avoiding a flood from the executive washroom.)

3

Coding Techniques—The Eyes Have It

When you engage in your favorite sport, all of your senses, emotions and feelings come into play. With the sense of sight, you measure distance between ball and cup as you line up that clutch birdie putt. With the sense of sound, you hear the solid smack of the tennis ball making contact with the sweet spot of the racket as you finally groove that troublesome backhand. With the sense of touch, you feel the perfect release of the bowling ball, knowing it will have just the right amount of spin and create just the right amount of pin action to roll that 10th frame strike. And so it is with your emotions and feelings, as you psyche yourself to excel, self-talk yourself to make the big play, pump up the adrenalin, prelive the sweetness of victory.

Your mind is like a video tape machine. It has the ability to record, store and play back all of this sensory information. What it lacks is an orderly system of storage and an efficient method of retrieval. Without such a system, it is like having a huge video-tape library of good and bad recordings haphazardly stored with no system of indexing or labeling that enables you to select the quality recordings you'd like to play back.

SyberVision provides the missing link. With the simple coding techniques explained in this chapter, you will learn how to process, store and efficiently recall this sensory information for consistent stroke or skill execution. Based on patterns of eye movements, SyberVision's coding technique provides a practical and logical system for the input and retrieval of sensory information.

Whenever you draw upon neurologically stored sensory memory, the eyes have a revealing pattern of movement that shows from which area of the brain you are retrieving these stored data. "His eyes gave him away," is a phrase much over-worked in detective fiction, but it has a strong ring of truth. Customs inspectors, police interrogators, clinical psychologists—persons involved in eliciting information from others—know that the eyes are windows to the mind. The eyes are unconscious betrayors of our emotions; they can signal to the trained or perceptive observer the way we think and feel.

The SyberVision Sensory Eye Shift Codes (see illustration), were designed to associate desired actions in sports with distinct movements of the eyes and to key those actions into the brain at all sensory levels. Using specific eye shifts, you will create door knobs, or entry codes, to each of the sensory areas of the brain. These codes will provide easy access to your mental storehouse, opening up areas of the brain for retention, activation and/or creation of high quality performance memory.

EYE SHIFT CODES

The following codes are designed for the right-handed person. If you are left-handed, the most common tendency is for the field of *visual* processing to be the reverse of that for the right-hand dominant person (reverse the two upper eye shifts *only*) while everything else remains the same as for the right-handed person.

1. Visual memory. When you draw from visual memory, recalling, for example, a golf instructor demonstrating the placement of the feet when hitting short-iron shots, or a tennis pro teaching you correct follow-through, your eyes shift naturally to the UPPER LEFT.

2. Constructed visual images. When you are creating new input for your mental storehouse—putting things together that are not reality, such as visually preliving an upcoming sports event by imagining yourself reading a newspaper story describing yourself winning that event—your eyes will shift to the UPPER RIGHT.

3. Auditory memory. This is your storehouse of remembered sounds—the crunch of your skis cutting into fresh powder snow, the echoing rattle of falling pins as you make a strike. Your eye shift is LATERAL LEFT.

4. Constructed sounds. This eye-movement pattern, a fine tool for composers and writers, comes into play when you are creating sounds and words. You might conjure in your mind's "ear," for example, the congratulatory yells of your teammates as you hear your bat solidly crunch the ball as you drive in the winning run in the bottom of the last inning of an upcoming baseball or softball game. Your eye shift is LATERAL RIGHT.

5. Emotional memory and feelings. When you recall feelings associated with a specific performance, your eyes shift to the LOWER LEFT position.

6. Motion memory and body sensation recall. When you use this eye pattern, you are activating kinesthetic recall, summoning the area of the brain that recalls body motion and

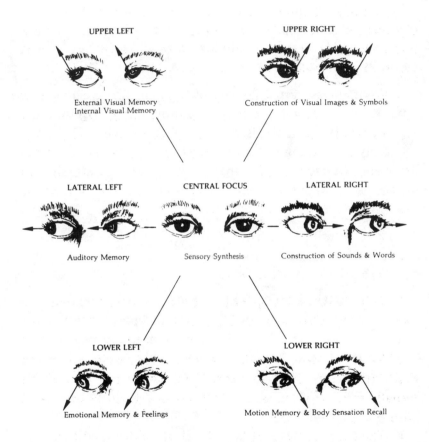

SyberVision Sensory Eye Shift Codes for a right-handed person

feeling, touch and muscle movement. Use it to recall and sense the fluid motion of that powerful serve you delivered the last time you aced an opponent. Shift your eyes LOWER RIGHT.

7. Sensory synthesis. This is the eye movement to bring it all together, after you have coded in each of the senses, emotions and feelings. It is the synthesis of all your senses working in harmony. Use a CENTRAL FOCUS for the eyes.

While these eye shifts are distinct movements in the directions indicated, they are fleeting, almost imperceptible movements. In most persons, however, they are discernible to the careful observer. To test this out for yourself, use the following coding questionnaire. As you draw from your memory storehouse to answer each of the questions, have someone watch your eye movements. Or try these questions on someone else and confirm for yourself the eye patterns we have charted as your subject activates the various areas of the brain.

THE SYBERVISION SENSORY EYE SHIFT CODE CHARTING QUESTIONNAIRE

1. Visual memory. Think of a relative or friend whom you don't frequently see. As clearly and as vividly as possible visually recall from memory the following features associated with that person:
   a. The exact contour of face, head, shoulders and body.
   b. The exact style, length of step and posture in walking.
   c. Characteristic facial expressions, smile, frown, laugh.
   d. A common item of clothing with colors the person often wears.

2. Constructed visual images. Create in your mind the following images as clearly and as vividly as possible:

a. Picture a bright yellow Volkswagen convertible that has flattened tires and is being used for a bubble bath—by a red-winged chimpanzee with a giraffe's neck and an elephant's trunk.

b. Have the red-winged chimp with a giraffe's neck and an elephant's trunk turn the car upside down to drain out the water.

c. Imagine your hybrid chimp in the same Volkswagon convertible climbing up a steep hill.

d. Imagine the car going out of control. Look at the panic on the chimp's face. See the car crash through a house owned by a hippopotamus sleeping in a waterbed.

3. Auditory memory. Recall from your experience the following sounds as clearly as possible:

a. The clapping of hands in fervent applause.

b. The whistle of a locomotive on a cold winter's morning.

c. The sound of a car passing by in the rain. You don't see the car; you are in a house.

d. The sound of steam escaping from a covered pot.

e. The night call of a prowling alley cat.

4. Constructed sounds. Mentally create the following sounds as clearly as possible:

a. A hoarse dog with a stuttering bark.

b. The sound of your name being announced over the PA system of a filled stadium as the singer of the National Anthem.

c. Howard Cosell's voice over the radio citing a newsworthy accomplishment of yours.

d. Create a language of your own and mentally sound out the translation of the following words: *talk, smell, wood, water.*

5. Emotional memory and feelings. Think of the following emotions you have experienced and mentally recreate them as clearly as possible:

    a. Anger.

    b. Fear.

    c. Confidence.

    d. Sudden joy.

    e. Sadness.

6. Motion memory and body sensation recall. Try to imagine, as clearly as possible, the feeling you would experience as you touch each of the following objects or perform each of the following actions. Try to capture, in your mind's eye, the sensations you would experience in your arms, legs, hands, feet, etc.

    a. The cold, wet sand.

    b. Rubbing against the fur of a cat.

    c. The tingling coldness of an icy bath.

    d. The sting of an inoculating shot in the arm or the rump.

    e. Drawing a square on paper.

    f. Running up a steep hill.

    g. Kicking a can as you slowly walk away.

    h. Jumping over a running brook.

You will be using these codes throughout the SyberVision program as you work at increasing your proficiency at a sport. Reverting to our door-knob analogy, you will use these codes to get into and out of your mind as you build your own video bank of superior athletic performance and as you draw upon that stored memory. Use the same eye-shift code to get in and out of your mind, just as you would a door knob.

An untrained person uses these codes haphazardly and imperfectly. With the SyberVision program you will learn to use them automatically and effectively. To accomplish this, of course, takes discipline and practice. It also requires the ability to relax fully and concentrate completely.

Ken Margerum demonstrating the
SyberVision Sensory Eye Shift Codes
for a right-handed person

Studies show that the brain barely distinguishes between actual performance and perceived performance. When we use the various muscle groups, they are powered electro-neurologically. The brain emits an electrical impulse that travels down the spinal column and then shoots out to the muscles and activates the chemical that causes the muscles to contract. If the muscles are not relaxed (oxygenated), or if they are in a state of tension (lack of oxygen), the codes you are putting into the brain will not have the opportunity to work effectively. Tension creates roadblocks to physical performance; relaxation enhances performance.

For this reason, the programs of Syber-Relaxation and Syber-Concentration detailed in the following chapters are essential if you are serious about improving your performance at your favorite sports. Use these programs in conjunction with the eye shift codes to make the brain more receptive to sensory information.

You'll learn to use the techniques to build a rich reservoir of superior athletic performance as you store sensory memories, recall them during performance and even play back your own past performances, editing out the flaws and weaknesses in your game for future improvements. In effect, you will be building a pyramid of performance in your mind, taking that low proficiency you now have and gradually enlarging it.

You'll also find that the ability to process sensory information efficiently and that enhanced powers of relaxation and concentration will have incremental benefits in other areas of your life. They can help you in your work, in your studies, in any creative endeavors, in mastering new techniques and skills—in fact, to help you realize your life goals.

4

Syber-Relaxation

"Relax! You can do it! Just get out there and relax!" How often have you heard a coach yell this or similar advice as he sends in a player to perform in a clutch situation? It's an admonition commonly heard in sports, from the little league right up to the majors. Usually, it achieves just the opposite of its intended effect.

Faced with a pressure situation and with the coach's advice echoing through his mind, the athlete desperately tries to force relaxation. He succeeds only in creating more performance-sapping tension, because as he grapples to control his pent-up anxieties blood flow becomes restricted and muscles get tighter. As a result, the kind of fluid movement that is essential to consistent performance becomes blocked out. The athlete is disappointed when he fails to deliver. The coach is upset because his player "choked." Yet it was the coach who had become a catalyst for creating tension because he had instructed his player to do something that the athlete had not been trained to do. Among the millions of athletes who engage in sports, few have truly masted the art of relaxation—the ability to enrich muscle tissue with oxygenated blood for fluid, responsive, cat-like movements. The athlete is unable to relax because he has no operational definition of what relaxation is.

Our system of Syber-Relaxation detailed in this chapter will provide you with a vivid working definition of relaxation. You will learn how it feels to have your muscles primed with oxygen-rich blood as you reach a totally relaxed state. You will learn how to summon this relaxation at will. Through a technique that uses eye-shift patterns, color cues and the application and release of tension throughout various muscle groups, you will learn a discipline for attaining a high level of relaxation. If you work at these exercises as prescribed, you will find that the ability to relax—whenever and wherever you need to—eventually will become a conditioned reflex. Total relaxation will come to you, quite literally, in the blink of an eye.

Relaxation is the foundation of consistent sport performance. Without it, you cannot expect to make your muscles respond fluidly and automatically to the intent of your mind. An athlete without the ability to relax is like a builder trying to construct a high-rise on a bed of shifting sand. No matter how talented the architect, how excellent the drawings and blueprints, how skilled the builder, if the conditions are not right— if the foundation is not stable—the project will not succeed.

When you apply the techniques of Syber-Relaxation, you are creating conditions that are right—a solid foundation—for the neuro-muscular coding of memory. Oxygen is the life force of muscle tissue. When the muscles are relaxed, a rich supply of oxygenated blood flows freely into the muscle tissue. If an athlete is experiencing muscle-binding tension—even imperceptible tension—this blood flow becomes restricted, curtailing supple movement and endurance.

For a graphic demonstration of this oxygenation process, try a simple experiment. Clench your fist and slowly flex your forearm and bicep muscles. Gradually build the tension in your arm and then hold it for a count of seven to 10 seconds. Then,

Muscle tension: the clenched fist experiment

quickly release the pressure. The feeling of warmth that flows through your arm is caused by the revitalizing flow of oxygenated blood into the muscles. Through the exercises in this chapter, you will learn how to capture this feeling of warmth and associate it with a relaxed state.

Another example of the oxygenation process and its vital role in relaxation is deep breathing exercises. Picture the tennis player about to receive a match-point serve that could eliminate him from competition. As he waits with racket poised, you can see his chest slowly rise and fall in a pattern of deep breathing. You know that he is trying to relax, trying to gain control of a tense, critical moment during which he cannot afford a mistake.

That tennis player is using the oxygenation principle. Every time he takes a deep breath and then exhales, oxygen is quickly assimilated into the bloodstream and sent surging throughout the body. This blood flow creates that feeling of relaxed warmth as it dissolves tension.

The Syber-Relaxation exercises that follow are designed to instill a mental discipline of relaxation. Eventually, that regimen will become automatic. You will be able to distill the entire process and oxygenate your muscle tissue simply by using the eye-shift codes and by recalling a series of color cues. However, as you put yourself through the daily relaxation exercises on your way to creating the ability to relax reflexively, you will acquire a sharpening of your skills of concentration.

Concentration and relaxation go hand-in-hand as essential ingredients of the personal equation that brings consistent sports performance. Concentration is the ability to focus your thought processes into a narrow channel, to block out unrelated thoughts, feelings, background noise and other environmental distractions. To develop the high level of relaxation that is your goal it is important to master the mental discipline of concentration. Then, when you are in a completely relaxed state, your body will react to your mind and your mind will react to your body. The following exercises will help you develop these skills.

SYBER-RELAXATION EXERCISES

Just after the turn of the century, Russian physiologist Ivan Petrovich Pavlov discovered the phenomenon of "the conditioned reflex." In his famous experiments, dogs were fed to the sound of a bell. They became so conditioned to this routine that eventually the mere sounding of the bell—even when not accompanied by feeding—was sufficient to cause the dogs to salivate. Recent research and biofeedback training shows that just about any autonomic (spontaneous) response can be conditioned. We can condition ourselves to respond to a cue or symbol. If that cue or symbol is associated in the mind with a certain body response, then flashing that code into the mind will activate the desired body response.

In the Syber-Relaxation program we use colors as cues—a separate color to activate each of three body zones. In conjunction with these color cues, we employ neuromuscular eye codes.

Eye codes are used to view each body region from two perspectives: 1. from a kinesthetic perspective—how it feels; 2. from a visual perspective—how it looks. Eye codes also are used in association with each of our three colors. You will practice mentally projecting a burst of color into the corresponding body zone to associate that color with the release of tension and the warm, relaxed feeling caused by the rush of oxygenated blood into the muscle tissue.

Body Zones and Colors

For the purposes of the Syber-Relaxation program, the body has been arbitrarily divided into three basic zones, each with its own individual muscle groups. Each of these zones is associated with a color, as follows:

Syber Zone 1. LOWER TORSO: right leg, left leg, buttocks
Color: RED
Syber Zone 2. UPPER TORSO: abdomen, chest, right arm, left arm, shoulder blades, back
Color: ORANGE
Syber Zone 3. HEAD: forehead and scalp, eyes, cheeks and nose, jaw and throat, back of neck
Color: YELLOW

It is important that you are able to close your eyes and mentally recall each of these colors. After a little practice, you

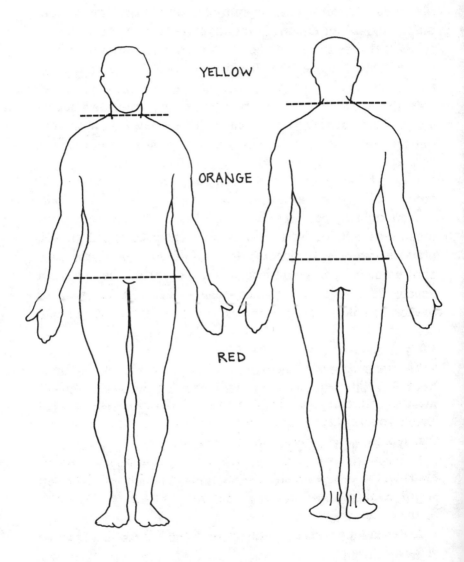

Syber Vision body zones

will find you will be able to do this quite easily. However, do not expect the color to blaze into the mind. Very few persons are such keen visualizers. Nor is this necessary. Simply try to recall in your mind a sense of what each color looks like.

As an aid to the recall of each color, we have in our California SyberVision training room one-foot-square panels representing each of the colors used for cueing relaxation and concentration. You might wish to duplicate this at home by temporarily mounting color panels on the wall in a corner of your rec room, study or bedroom—whatever quiet place free from noise, distraction and interruption that you choose to do your relaxation exercises. For a smaller, portable aid, we suggest clipping color chips from a paint dealer's sample sheet and mounting each color on a separate 4x5 index card. Or you may wish to use objects to help you cue into each color—an apple, an orange, a lemon, for the colors red, orange and yellow. This is acceptable, although less desirable because the objects represent an additional crutch that you later will discard.

Color Recall Exercise

As a preliminary step to beginning the actual relaxation exercise, practice this simple exercise for color recall. It will enable you quickly to summon to mind each of the three colors that represent the three zones of the body.

1. With an upper left eye shift (to input visual memory), focus on the wall panel or color chip for the color red. Imagine your eyes as the zoom lens of a camera focusing in on the center of the color sample.

2. Repeat this process for the color orange; then for the color yellow.

3. Close your eyes and rest for a moment to allow your mind to calm itself and to allow the optic nerves to complete the processing of the actual color images.

4. Shift your eyes upper left (visual memory recall); then, with your eyes closed, recall in turn each of the three colors. Remember, don't expect a flood of color. Simply try to remember what each color looked like.

The more you practice this exercise, the easier it will become quickly to recall these colors. The concept of recalling colors is the first step toward establishing the ability to relax as a conditioned reflex. It also is a honing tool that will help you put a cutting edge on your powers of concentration.

Preparation for Syber-Relaxation

1. Find yourself a comfortable chair or couch. Ideal is a reclining chair that adjusts to a relaxed, feet-up position. A chaise-longue also works well, as does a waterbed—or even an air mattress placed on the floor. The idea is to support the body weight totally. You don't want to be able to feel or sense any part of the body supporting itself, because this can cause tension in and of itself.

2. Dress comfortably, perhaps in a warm-up suit, a loose-fitting robe or tee-shirt and shorts. The aim is to avoid any object that you can sense as being weighty or binding. Be sure to remove shoes, glasses, watch, rings, belt and any other similar objects. You need to feel completely unrestricted.

3. Sit, recline or lie in such a position, with your feet up and arms at your side, that your body is totally supported by the chair or couch.

4. As a warm-up and sharpening exercise for color recall, mentally recall the colors for the three body zones. Using the upper left eye shift code, close your eyes and slowly bring to mind the colors red, orange and yellow, in that order.

Now, you are ready to begin associating the colors with the relaxation of various zones of the body. The following exercises are designed to enhance that color association—to make it a conditioned reflex and, at the same time, to provide a clear

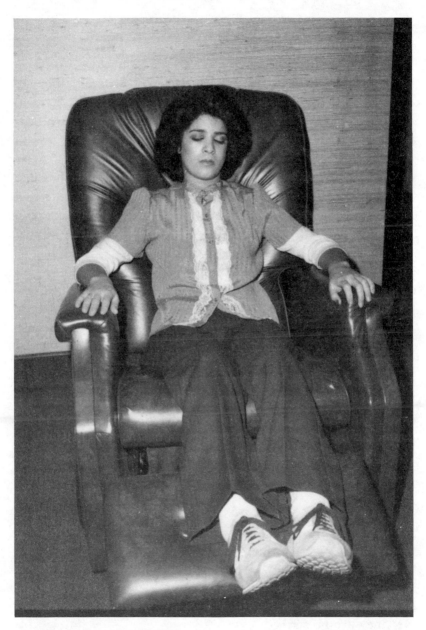

An ideal position for SyberRelaxation

distinction between the feeling of tension and the warm glow of relaxation.

Complete the following Basic Exercise twice each day for a minimum of one week, ideally, for two weeks. If possible, do the exercise first thing in the morning while you are still fresh, and in early evening. Certainly avoid this exercise close to bedtime or you may find yourself becoming so relaxed that you will end up by activating your color cues to condition sleep! After one or two weeks, switch to the abbreviated Intermediate Exercise (see instructions). However, you should continue as a maintenance program to complete the basic exercise once a week. Make it a lifetime habit. You will find that the results make it worthwhile!

Note: If, during the tension portion of the exercise, you experience a cramp—the legs are particularly susceptible— don't panic. Instead, try a visual technique that many athletes who enroll in our SyberVision training programs find useful. Imagine the constricted muscle as a hard, cold ball of butter. Then imagine a warm flow of blood flooding into the muscle, melting the butter, dissolving the cramp.

Also, if you have any kind of injury—back, shoulder, leg, etc.—be sure not to tense that area beyond the threshold of pain. Remember, pain is the body's warning to cease and desist.

BASIC EXERCISE

Syber Zone 1 (LOWER TORSO: RED)
Note: If you are right-handed, proceed as follows. If you are left-handed, begin with left leg, then right leg, then proceed with instructions. Southpaws also should reverse upper left and upper right eye shift codes—but **only** those two codes—whenever they are prescribed.

1. With upper left eye shift, key into the conditioning color RED.

2. With lower right eye shift, mentally isolate the right leg. Focus your attention onto the leg and mentally scan it from the tips of the toes all the way up to the hip area—mentally "feeling" your toes, heel, ankle, calf, knee, hamstring and thigh area.

3. Slowly build up tension in the right leg by tightening the leg muscles, beginning with the foot—balling it as if it was a fist—and progressively tightening up to the thigh area. You'll feel the tension build as circulation becomes restricted and muscles are starved of oxygen.

4. Hold the tension for 7-10 seconds.

5. With the upper right eye shift, quickly release the tension throughout the leg and simultaneously project the color RED into the leg. Imagine you are flooding the leg with a burst of color from a space-fantasy beam gun. It is important to time this mental beaming of color to coincide with the point of release of the tension. Again, be sure that this release of tension is a quick release.

6. With a lower right eye shift focus your entire attention on the glow of relaxation that flows into the leg as the result of the flow of oxygenated blood into the muscles. Maintain this focus for 30-40 seconds as you capture that feeling of oxygenation of muscle tissue—that sense of relaxation flooding in. Bask in this warm feeling of relaxation as tension melts away and the oxygen-starved muscles hungrily soak up nourishment.

7. Proceed to left leg and follow the same procedure (steps 2 to 6) as you did for the right leg.

8. With a lower right eye shift mentally isolate from the rest of the body the buttocks area. Mentally scan this area for feeling and sensation.

9. Follow steps 3-6, adapting them to the buttocks area.

Apply tension by bearing down into the seat of the chair, pushing muscle against muscle isometrically.

10. With an upper right eye shift, construct a mental picture of a red mist, vapor or fog swirling around the head. Sense this red mist circulating in front of the forehead and nose.

11. Slowly inhale a long, deep stream of this red-mist-filled air simultaneously through each nostril, totally filling the chest cavity to capacity. Hold this breath for a slow count of five.

12. With a lower right eye shift, slowly release the air back through the nostrils and sense the feeling of oxygen saturating the muscles of the lower torso. This "sensing" should extend from 45-60 seconds to heighten the sensation of relaxation flowing down through the legs and buttocks area. Concentrate on and stay with this feeling.

Syber Zone 2 (Upper Torso: ORANGE)

1. With upper left eye shift recall the color ORANGE. This is the activation color for relaxation/oxygenation conditioning of the upper torso.

2. Slowly work through each of the following muscle groups by applying steps 2 through 6, Syber Zone 1 to each group. In other words, for each muscle group you will isolate, scan, tense, release tension and project the color ORANGE—all with the eye shifts previously indicated for Syber Zone 1. Note: If you are left-handed, reverse the processing order for the right arm and left arm.

   a. Abdominal area—to create tension, tighten the muscles of the diaphram, as though preparing to take a punch in the stomach;

   b. Chest—press one side of the chest against the other, pushing down and across;

   c. Right arm—clench fist and tense forearm, bicep and tricep muscles up to the shoulders;

d. Left arm—tense as for right arm;

e. Shoulder blades (back)—bring the shoulder blades together, tighten the mass of muscles in the back.

3. Proceed to deep breathing exercise as outlined in steps 10 through 12, Syber Zone 1, using the color ORANGE instead of red to create the circulating cloud of mist.

Syber Zone 3 (Head: YELLOW)

1. With upper left eye shift, key into the color YELLOW. This is the relaxation/oxygenation conditioning color for the head, scalp and neck areas.

2. Slowly work through each of the following muscle groups by applying steps 2 through 6, Syber Zone 1 to each group:

a. Forehead and scalp—to create tension, raise the eyebrows to meet the scalp and push the scalp down toward the eyebrows in opposition—as if you were furrowing your brow.

b. Eyes, nose and cheeks—with eyes closed, squint gently and at the same time wrinkle the nose, pushing out the tip and bringing the upper lip up toward the nose;

c. Jaw, chin and throat—push chin and jaw straight out, bite teeth together and pull back corners of mouth, tighten throat;

d. Neck—pull chin slowly downward toward chest (without touching chest).

3. Proceed to deep breathing exercise as outlined in steps 10 through 12, Syber Zone 1, using the color YELLOW instead of red to create the circulating cloud of mist.

Conclusion—Reinforcement

1. With upper left eye shift, slowly reverse the colors, working down from yellow to orange to red and associating each color with its specific body zone. Complement this association with a lower right eye shift.

2. With a center eye shift, slowly open eyes and shake out

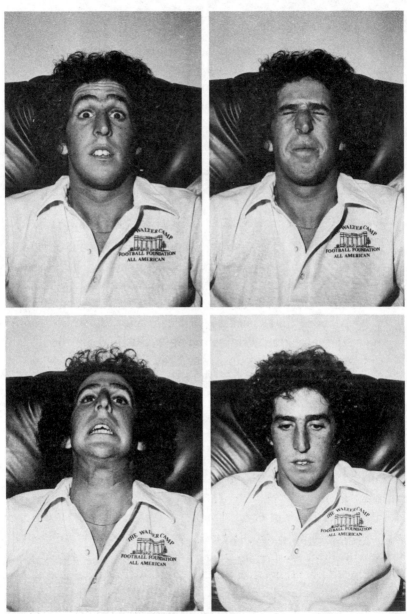

SyberZone 3 conditioning exercises

Concluding eye shifts in SyberRelaxation

arms and legs. At this point you will be relaxed, vitalized and clear-minded.

The object of this exercise is, as we have stated, to make relaxation a conditioned reflex. Over a period of four to six weeks, you will first become totally at home with the Basic Exercise, then learn to pare it down to an abbreviated form. Finally, you will find that you need the full exercise program only as a once-a-week reinforcement. When you reach that point, relaxation will come quickly merely by using the upper left eye shift and quickly zeroing in on each of the three color cues. This takes only seconds. It means that the ability to relax has, indeed, become a conditioned reflex. It is, however, a process that cannot be hurried. It must happen naturally. And the time it takes for relaxation to become an automatic response will vary with the individual. So please give it time.

This applies to the entire SyberVision process of which relaxation is a part, albeit an important part—indeed, the foundation. Allow the SyberVision process to happen naturally. By forcing yourself you only create an environment of tension and anxiety. SyberVision is not a quick fix, overnight success program. To enjoy the benefits of the program you must work hard.

The initial weeks of SyberVision training can be compared to the germination period of an oak tree. The seed is planted and takes many months to germinate. If, out of impatience on the part of the sower, the seed is uprooted to check its growth, the germination process will stop. Looking at the uprooted seed, it appears the same as it was before it was planted. But below the surface wonderful things were taking place that would have allowed the seed to become a mighty oak, if only given the chance to grow. So, be patient. It takes time and hard work to change old self-defeating habits and ingrain new ones. Let it happen naturally. But instead of months (like the acorn) your germination and growth process will begin to unfold in a matter of weeks.

INTERMEDIATE EXERCISE

After you have followed the basic exercise program twice daily for a minimum of one week, ideally two weeks, you should be ready to switch to the abbreviated version. Follow the intermediate program for four to six weeks, substituting, one day a week, the full basic exercise program. From this point on, the full basic exercise program should become a once-a-week habit. For the intermediate exercise program, you simply eliminate or condense portions of the basic exercise program, as follows:

1. Recall each of the three body zones as a whole and scan the

entire zone instead of each muscle group individually.

2. Eliminate the tensing and relaxation procedure—simply scan each of the three body zones and flood in the appropriate conditioning color.

3. Eliminate the breathing exercise that follows each of the body zones.

Remember: Follow all instructions as before for the eye shift codes.

ADVANCED EXERCISE

When you reach this stage, after six to eight weeks, you have achieved your goal of making relaxation a conditioned reflex that you are able to summon at will. To produce the desired state of relaxation, simply:

1. With an upper left eye shift, cue into the activating color RED.

2. Repeat for the color ORANGE.

3. Repeat for the color YELLOW.

5

Syber-Concentration

In an age of electronic data processing, you already own the world's most sophisticated computer—the human brain. It has the capacity to record and store vast amounts of information relating to past and current events—things you've seen, done, felt, heard, read. In short, all of your life's experiences. As to the goal of improving your performance at your favorite sport, your brain already carries stored data on all of the correct body actions and all of the feelings, emotions, sights and sounds that accompany those perfectly-executed movements. It carries an electronically encoded blueprint of the fluid golf swing, the perfectly-timed tennis stroke, the well-delivered bowling ball, the effortless downhill ski run.

The big problem with this wonderful human computer is the manner in which it typically processes data. Lacking a logical, orderly system, input is random, storage haphazard. As a result, the timely retrieval of data becomes a matter of chance. Mixed with all of the vital facts and figures are hordes of useless trivia. Locked in with the memories of those five glorious times in 100 when you executed a perfect movement in your sport are imprints of the 95 times you flubbed.

How often have you groped for a word or a telephone number, struggled to recall a fact or detail of information that you know is buried somewhere in the recesses of your mind? It is the same thing with those well-executed sports movements. You know that you have those muscle-memory imprints stored somewhere in the data banks of that complex computer of yours. You once actually executed those perfect strokes and have watched others make them countless times. Stored somewhere in your mind are the memories of these outstanding sports performances. The problem is, you simply can't call up this information when you need it. You can't seem to hit the right button for retrieval. It's like owning a magnificent computer but having no programmer to help you input data systematically, store it where it is easily found and retrieve it whenever it is needed.

This is what concentration is all about. Simply defined, concentration is the ability to select and respond to relevant stimuli while closing out irrelevant stimuli. On a given day, one of your senses—sight, sound, touch, emotion—will be more accessible to your mind than will the other senses. Concentration is the ability to identify that predominant sense and use it as a single track to open up all of the storage banks of the mind.

With the SyberVision program, you will learn to be your own computer programmer. You'll discover how to effectively input coded memories of those desirable sports movements—how they look, feel and sound, plus all of the emotions, sensations and feelings associated with them. You'll learn how to systematically store these muscle-memory imprints in your mind. And you'll acquire a technique for stimulating and activating them during actual play. In effect, you'll be building a computer bank of excellence in sports performance. You'll have "on tape" a growing storehouse of positive muscle memory that you eventually will be able to draw upon automatically.

You'll find that this memory bank of positive performance

that you are gradually building will allow you to expand your consistency level at your sport. You will notice yourself begin to trim strokes from your golf handicap, add points to your bowling average or show comparable improvement at whatever sport you play. That five percent consistency level will begin to balloon to 10 percent, then 15 percent, and on up. More and more those fundamentals of your sport will become automatic.

Your training to become a skilled programmer of that computer inside your head has already begun. The eye-shift patterns described earlier in this book provide fast and logical access to your mind's data storage banks. These eye codes are your own personal "computer language." Like the dial on a radio, they tune your brain into the right wavelength. With each eye-shift pattern you gain direct and open access to a separate storage compartment of the mind.

Even a late-generation computer with a well-designed program will be stymied if the plant and machinery it controls is not functioning efficiently. By using the relaxation exercises detailed in the preceding chapter, your body—your personal plant and machinery—will be perfectly primed to respond to instructions generated by your mental computer. Oxygenation of the nervous tissue of the muscles is the oil which makes your machinery run smoothly. In a state of relaxation, your mind and body are able to work in harmony. When this occurs, your athletic skills become "grooved."

It is important to gain an understanding of how this mental computer functions. Knowing precisely in which areas of the mind certain kinds of information are stored will help you improve your muscle-memory storage and recall. To paraphrase a computer axiom: Easy in, easy out.

Functionally, the brain is divided into two sections, the left cerebral hemisphere and the right cerebral hemisphere. Separating the two sections is the corpus callosum, a structure of nervous tissue and fiber that acts as a bridge for the transfer of electrical impulses between the left and right cerebral hemispheres. This tissue allows for the coordinated interchange of information and functioning between the two hemispheres.

The **left cerebral hemisphere** is the cognitive side of the brain. Its role is rational and logical thinking and verbal and analytical functions. The left cerebral hemisphere is the essence of thinking man. In athletic competition, it is the side of the brain that handles strategy and planning as opposed to pure technique and repetitive skills. It is this cognitive capacity that sets man into a higher order than the animals.

The **right cerebral hemisphere** handles non-verbal functions and the processing of sensory information relating to sight, sound, touch and emotional memory. This is the side of the brain that man has in common with all animals. It is the source of instinctive, conditioned reflexes. In a lion, for example, the right-brain function is totally dominant. If the lion had the cognitive ability of man, its hunting effectiveness would be greatly reduced. It would be thinking about *how* to attack its prey rather than working from conditioned reflexes.

It is the right side of the brain that you will need to activate as you expand that level of playing consistency from the hypothetical five percent upward to 20 percent, 50 percent and beyond. In game situations, it is this right-side dominance that instinctively prompts the great running back to switch the football from one hand to the other away from the pursuing linebacker intent on jarring it loose. Working off the right side of the brain, the professional golfer executes a flawless swing hole after hole to drop approach shots unfailingly onto greens. Meanwhile, he is using the left side of his brain—the cognitive hemisphere—to contemplate pin placement, prevailing wind conditions and strategy involved in shooting for a downhill or uphill lie.

In contrast to the pro, the weekend athlete uses his cognitive abilities to think, not about playing strategy, but about the fundamentals of his game. Instead of letting the golf swing come naturally, he thinks about it and mentally reduces it to its component parts—thinking about back swing, hip action, wrist break, role of the arms, legs, etc. As a result, stress and tension build and, as relaxation falls apart, so does his game. He has become a victim of "paralysis by analysis."

Yet this reflexive ability to execute purely from stored memory is not the exclusive province of the professional or top amateur athlete. Even the weekend athlete will occasionally talk about experiencing a "groove" or a "flow" when everything went smoothly. This occurs when that person is totally relaxed and concentrated, oblivious to environmental distractions, allowing the right side of the brain to work naturally. Although this "groove" effect may occur rarely, it does occur. And, since it happens on occasion, it has the potential of occuring more often. And that's what Syber-Concentration is all about.

Its objective is to train your mind to become the initiator of fundamentally sound and consistent complex movement. A simple explanation of how the brain functions in regard to movement may be helpful. It gets back to our concept of mental "blueprints."

Dispersed throughout the brain are electro-chemical traces or patterns of previously performed movement. Every time we initiate a deliberate movement, we activate these stored patterns which, in turn, guide our movement. The movement is recorded simultaneously by the nervous system where it becomes a permanent part of the reservoir of stored memory patterns.

At first, any new movement must be consciously learned. After hundreds of hours of repetition the movement becomes automatic or habitual. (It requires approximately 400 hours of conscious repetition for a skill to become fully automatic.) Every time we initiate a walking action we don't instruct ourselves in the mechanics of walking. It occurs automatically and instinctively from memory.

As an illustration, let's look at what happens in the nervous system when the mind initiates the intent to walk:

This command is received in the motor cortex area of the brain in the form of an electronically-coded impulse. Within milliseconds the brain searches its memory for a model to imitate. Once the electronically-coded model is located, an electro-chemical representation of that model is routed to the spinal cord. The spinal cord then sends the code along the proper nervous pathways leading to the muscles that must act to perform the desired action. Close to the muscle, the electronic code triggers a chemical reaction which causes the muscle tissue to contract. The muscle contraction and all of the tiny muscular movements that are made in purposeful action are monitored by the cerebellum, the brain region that controls fine movement and coordination.

At this point, our Syber-Relaxation programs play an important role. If the muscle tissue which is responsible for the motion is enriched with oxygen and nutrients furnished by unrestricted blood flow, then the muscle contraction will be fluid, a pure representation of the original intent. In such a state the muscle is said to be "relaxed" or fluidly responsive. Should blood flow to the muscle be constricted, the action of the muscle will be rigid, thus causing a muscular response that will be an aberration from the original intent; the muscle is in a state of "negative tension."

Once the movement is completed, the individual analyzes the body sensation generated by the movement as being either fluid ("It felt good") or rigid ("It didn't feel right, something went wrong"). At the same time, the result of the movement is analyzed as being realized or unrealized. The individual then attaches a positive or negative psychological assessment to the movement. This assessment, along with a record of the physiological state of the muscle tissue and the original electrical code of the movement, then is fed back to the brain where it is stored as a newly-coded electrical pattern for future recall.

The quality of the movement (whether or not it was consistent with the intention) is influenced by three inter-related variables: 1. the quality of the electrical memory pattern; 2. the state of muscle tension (whether or not the muscles are oxygenated); and 3. the psychological framework of the individual at the time of execution.

Weekend athletes are particularly vulnerable to psychological stress. All too often they may experience sensations of tightness in the arms and legs, pounding in the chest and stomach and the feeling of a "lump in the throat" that accompany a lack of confidence in the ability to perform consistently.

If the athlete has low self-esteem or lacks confidence to perform up to expectations, he or she will trigger, as a conditioned response, the stored memory patterns associated with that psychological state. Doubt in the ability to perform expresses itself physiologically. The doubt creates stress which causes the blood vessels that feed the muscle tissue to constrict. This constriction reduces the blood flow to the muscle, diverting it from the body's extremities (arms, legs, digits, head) to the body core (heart, abdomen) to provide the oxygen and nutrients necessary to fuel rapid mobilization in situations of "fight or flight." This self-doubt is interpreted by the body's physiology as fear and the body's responses act accordingly.

If you are to improve your athletic performance, you need to release yourself from this revolving door of tension building more tension, of poor quality movement begetting similar poor quality. You need to weed out those ragged, fuzzy areas in your mental data bank of muscle memory. Work on sharpening your system of input, storage and retrieval. Learn to concentrate.

Use the exercise program that follows in tandem with the Syber-Relaxation program detailed in the preceding chapter as a mental sports training program. By following the recommended schedule, you will condition yourself to concentrate as an automatic response. These exercises will help you create a grooved and singleminded channel of thought through which the electronically-encoded impulses or "blueprints" of desirable movement can travel unimpeded to activate relaxed and primed muscle tissue for precise and coordinated movement.

SYBER-CONCENTRATION
CONDITIONING EXERCISE

This exercise is an add-on to the Syber-Relaxation exercise. It begins only after you have completed the first phase of the Syber-Relaxation program—when you have graduated from the full-blown Basic Exercise to the abbreviated Intermediate Exercise. As you will recall, the Basic Exercise in the Syber-Relaxation program is suggested as a twice-daily regimen for a minimum of one week, ideally for two weeks. Once you are beyond this stage, simply tag the Syber-Concentration program on the end.

Cerebral Zones and Colors

As explained earlier in this chapter, the Syber-Concentration program divides the brain into three basic zones. These complement the three basic body zones previously described (Syber Zones 1, 2, and 3—see Chapter 4). Color cues for the brain are as follows:

Syber Zone 4. LEFT CEREBRAL HEMISPHERE—rational thinking, verbal functions, strategy building.
Color: GREEN

Syber Zone 5. RIGHT CEREBRAL HEMISPHERE—non-verbal functions, sensory (visual, sound, touch, emotional) memory storage and processing.
Color: BLUE

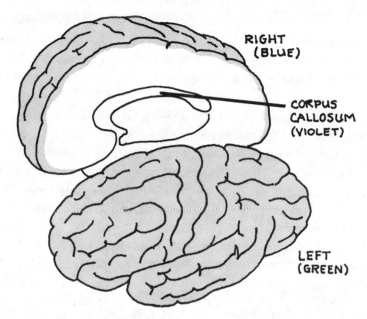

RIGHT
(BLUE)

CORPUS
CALLOSUM
(VIOLET)

LEFT
(GREEN)

The cerebral hemispheres

Syber Zone 6. CORPUS CALLOSUM—nervous tissue and fiber that acts as a bridge for the transfer of electrical impulses between the left and right cerebral hemispheres. This tissue allows for the coordinated interchange of information and functioning between the two hemispheres.
Color: VIOLET

As an aid to the recall of these color cues, you may wish to follow the suggestions made in the previous chapter. Until you get them down pat and are able to bring them instantly to mind, use wall-mounted panels, index cards with paint color chips or even associated objects. For the latter, we suggest: grass, sky and the bloom of an African violet for the colors green, blue and violet.

BASIC EXERCISE

Because this exercise is simply added to the Intermediate Exercise in the Syber-Relaxation program, you already will have taken all of the preparatory steps. You will be ensconced in that overstuffed chair (by now, your SyberVision chair!) or couch, dressed comfortably in loose-fitting clothing with all binding or restricting objects removed.

Here, then, is your basic Syber-Concentration exercise:

1. Complete the Syber-Relaxation Intermediate Exercise (see page 56), working through each of the three body zones—lower torso, upper torso, head—using the color codes red, orange, yellow.

2. Having completed the conditioning of Syber Zones 1, 2 and 3, work on Syber Zones 4, 5, and 6 as follows:

Syber Zone 4 (Left Cerebral Hemisphere; GREEN)
a. **Upper Left Eye-Shift Code (ESC)**. Recall the color GREEN. This is the conditioning color for access into the functions of the left cerebral hemisphere of the brain.
b. **Lower Right ESC.** Focus your attention on the left side of the brain. Mentally scan the left brain area.
c. **Upper Right ESC.** Beam the color GREEN to the left brain area, gradually flooding the area with GREEN.
d. **Lower Right ESC.** Sense a sharpening of concentration, of thinking prowess, a clarity and precision of mind.

Syber Zone 5 (Right Cerebral Hemisphere; BLUE)
a. **Upper Left ESC.** Recall the color BLUE. This is the conditioning color for access into the functions of the right cerebral hemisphere of the brain.
b. **Lower Right ESC.** Focus your attention on the right side of the brain. Mentally scan the right side of the brain.
c. **Upper Right ESC.** Beam the color BLUE to the right brain

area, gradually flooding the area with BLUE.

d. **Lower Right ESC.** Sense a sharpening of concentration, a peaking of the senses, a clarity and precision of mind.

Syber Zone 6 (Corpus Callosum: VIOLET)

a. **Upper Left ESC.** Recall the color VIOLET. This is the conditioning color for access to the corpus callosum for the integration of functions of the left and right cerebral hemispheres.

b. **Lower Right ESC.** Focus your attention on the sheath of nervous tissue joining the left and right cerebral hemispheres. Scan the area from the front of the brain to the back, following the pathway of this connective tissue.

c. **Upper Right ESC.** Beam the color VIOLET to the corpus callosum material, gradually flooding the area with VIOLET.

d. **Lower Right ESC.** Sense a sharpening of concentration, a peaking of the powers of thought and the senses, a total clarity and precision of mind.

Conclusion—Reinforcement

a. **Upper Left ESC.** Slowly reverse the colors, working down from VIOLET to RED, associating each color with its specific body zone. Complement each association with a **Lower Right ESC.**

b. **Central Focus ESC.** Slowly open the eyes and shake out the arms and legs. At this point you will be relaxed, vitalized and clear-minded.

ADVANCED EXERCISE

After six to eight weeks, relaxation/oxygenation and sharp concentration should become a conditioned reflex that you are able to summon at will. At this point, you simply cue into the activating color with an upper left eye shift, progressing from

RED through VIOLET for each of the six Syber Zones. In other words, your *total exercise* for relaxation and concentration is as follows:

1. **Upper Left ESC.** Cue into the activating color RED.
2. Repeat for the color ORANGE.
3. Repeat for the color YELLOW.
4. Repeat for the color GREEN.
5. Repeat for the color BLUE.
6. Repeat for the color VIOLET.

6

Your Television Laboratory of Learning

Every sports fan is aware of the far-reaching impact that television has upon sports. Televised sports has become a mega-buck business. It affects scheduling, players' salaries, the bottom-line profits of owners of professional franchises, and even in some cases the rules of the game. Television transforms sports figures into superstars and national heroes. It has the power to project an obscure sport into national prominence.

Television also can have a big impact on sports performance —*your* sports performance. We talked earlier in this book about the "SyberVision phenomenon" that probably most of us have experienced at one time or another. This occurs when a weekend athlete, after watching a televised sporting event— perhaps a tournament on the pro bowling, golf or tennis tours —goes out to play some hours later and finds that he or she is executing way above normal performance levels. This phenomenon, euphoric while it lasts, is the result of feedback from the television screen stimulating that five percent or so of fundamentally sound stored athletic memory that most of us have tucked away.

This feedback from television is a catalyst that affects all of the senses—sight, sound, touch, feelings, emotions. We remember some years ago an amateur soccer player intensely watching, the day before a key club match, a championship professional game on television. The following day, that amateur soccer player went out and played the game of his life—way above his usual performance level. Not only were his movements fluid, his passes crisp and accurate, but he was up emotionally, too, almost "hearing" the roar of the 80,000 spectators that had packed the stadium the day before, "feeling" the emotional high of the professional soccer players who had battled for the national title. The "SyberVision phenomenon" at work!

A more recent example is that of Andy Been, reserve-team tennis player at California State University at Hayward, who went through the SyberVision program. Watching video tapes on the television screen at the SyberVision headquarters of himself displaying perfect form with all the flaws and errors edited out, Been became so emotionally hyped that he would come away from SyberVision sessions muttering, "Here I come, Bjorn Borg." Been hasn't yet earned a match with Borg, but after SyberVision training he made a surprising break into the Cal State starting line-up and finished the season with a flawless record. Not a bad achievement for a player who had started the season as a bench-warmer!

In the case of the amateur soccer player and other weekend athletes who experience this feedback phenomenon, the effect is fleeting. The groove effect soon dissipates. The moments of glory pass and the player slips back into the old error-filled, tension-marred ways. In Been's case, the design of Syber-Vision training was to make those moments lasting, to build a useable reservoir of stored excellence. And that, too, is the object of this chapter. We are going to show you how to use your television set as a "living room laboratory of learning" to help you program excellence into your game.

Instead of passively viewing television coverage of your favorite sport, you will learn to use techniques of the Syber-Vision system to involve you in a valuable learning experience. They will enable you to plug the computer in your mind into the action on your television screen. And they will give you access to instructors that are the world's best in your sport. Imagine learning to adapt to your own game components of the powerful swing of Jack Nicklaus or the delicate putting touch of Nancy Lopez. Or how about incorporating into your tennis game elements of John McEnroe's devastating serve or Chris Evert Lloyd's winning backhand? Or perhaps you'd like to pick up on touring bowling pro Marshall Holman's aggressive delivery or on the downhill grace of skier Ingemar Stenmark.

Certainly, we can't claim to make you into another Jack Nicklaus or a Chris Evert Lloyd. Nor can we guarantee to make you club champion. But, if you follow the coding techniques described in this and the previous chapters, we can show you how to use television sports programs to build your proficiency level gradually, from that hypothetical five percent (five well-executed moves out of 100 attempts) to whatever higher level it is within your capability and within your will to reach. Instead of sitting back in front of the small screen sipping a beer, munching a sandwich and wistfully envying the par excellence flashing before you, you will learn to tap into that performance and use it to expand your computer bank of positive sports performance. Eventually, you will be able to incorporate much of it into your game.

Together, we're going to fill those computer storage banks in your mind with positive images. We are going to take sensory input from your television screen and put it into your memory at a frequency where it will resonate with previously stored memory and where it can be activated as needed when you go out to play the sport yourself.

TELEVISION CODING

Let's suppose you have consulted the TV program listings and that you have selected a sports telecast that you are going to watch. It may be one of the events on the Professional Golf Association tour, or perhaps tennis from Wimbledon or Forest Hills, or perhaps bowling's Tournament of Champions. You are going to settle back to watch this program, just as you usually do, but you are going to watch it as you never have before. You are going to watch it with all of your senses activated for sensory input and storage. You are going to select excerpts of that telecast—the sights, sounds and emotions attached to elements of play you want to incorporate into your own game—and put them onto your own video tape in your mind. Later, you are going to retrieve this mental video tape, mentally "replay" it in practice sessions and subsequently incorporate material that is imprinted on this tape into your game during competition.

But first, we suggest some fine tuning. Instead of trying to absorb, or input, the entire content of a sports telecast, concentrate on segments that relate to aspects of your game that you feel are most in need of improvement. Focus your viewing on two or three aspects of your game that need attention. Perhaps in golf you will want to work on your putting, your long or short irons, your fairway woods, your chipping, pitch-and-run or sand-trap play. In tennis, it may be the serve, the return of serve, backhand or forehand shots, or specific court play such as volleying at the net or executing the half-volley or overhead smash. In bowling, you may wish to concentrate on approach footwork, the release, the follow-through or cross-lane techniques for picking up spares. In any event, prior to your television encoding session make up your own short list of the most pressing deficiencies in your game and be ready to focus on those aspects of the play that will unfold on the television screen.

Another important point to keep in mind is the remarkable ability of the brain. It has the inherent capacity to take movement processed through the eyes and adapt that movement to your personal specifications. It works like a voltage regulator that accepts powerful house current and adapts it to power a tiny toy train.

This adaptive ability of the brain is important because it means that you don't have to scan the players parading by on your television screen, searching for a performer that closely matches your own physical dimensions. If you see an element of form on the screen that you can use—a particular golf swing or tennis stroke—you can go ahead and code into it regardless of how differently its practitioner may be built from yourself. It isn't critical, for example, if you are 5'8" and you focus on your television screen on the movements of an athlete who happens to be 6'2". Your brain has the ability to make this adjustment. It will take this visual and sensory input and adapt it to your biomechanical structure. Your brain knows your body best and it can take and store imprints of fundamental movements and adapt them to suit your own physical make-up. Thus, if you are small in stature and a similarly slightly-built golfer, such as the diminuitive Chi Chi Rodriguez, doesn't happen to appear on your TV screen, you still can focus on someone such as big Tom Weiskopf and let your brain custom-convert his swing to your smaller frame.

With these explanations, you now are ready to begin your first television coding experience. The procedure is as follows:

1. As with all SyberVision exercises, prepare yourself for input from television by getting comfortable. Settle yourself in that easy chair or couch with your shoes off, your feet up. You'll be dressed in comfortable, loose-fitting clothing, having

Your brain can custom-convert any sports movement

removed all restricting or binding objects—belt, glasses, watch, rings, etc. In other words, you are seeking absolute relaxation that will enable you to program yourself into a state of complete concentration, just as you do when going through your Syber-Relaxation and Syber-Concentration exercise routines (by now, they *should* be routine!). In fact, a prelude to receiving input from television is to put yourself through the relaxation/concentration program at the abbreviated advanced level (up to the color blue) as follows:

a. Using **upper left eye shift code,** cue into the color RED, the conditioning color to oxygenate the muscles of the lower torso.

b. Repeat for the color ORANGE, the conditioning color to oxygenate the muscles of the upper torso.

c. Repeat for the color YELLOW, the conditioning color to oxygenate the muscles of the facial area.

d. Repeat for the color GREEN, the conditioning color for access into the functions of the left cerebral hemisphere.

e. Repeat for the color BLUE, the conditioning color for access into the functions of the right cerebral hemisphere.

Once you have brought the color blue into the right cerebral hemisphere, slowly transfer that color to the center of the head. Start it out as a central pinpoint of color and allow it to slowly blossom and expand, becoming larger and larger, until you feel that your entire head, from the top of the scalp to the base of the neck, is filled with blue. At this point you are ready to code sensory information into the memory.

2. As you will recall from our discussion of eye-coding techniques (Chapter 3), each eye-shift pattern is associated with a specific sensory storage area of the brain—visual, auditory, emotional, kinesthetic. As you begin your input from television, you should first key into each of these areas to isolate each sense and sharpen it. It's like running through a checklist before using a piece of machinery as you briefly switch on

each part to be sure it is functioning properly.

At the beginning of your television coding session, spend about two minutes viewing the screen in each of the eye zones. Then watch the remainder of the program in a central eye focus, synthesizing all of the senses and concentrating on particular aspects of your game that you have earmarked for improvement. For this initial sensory sharpening process, spend two minutes in each eye zone in the following sequence:

a. **Upper left eye shift code.** This opens the memory for external visual storage; what the motion looks like when performed correctly—the fluid, easy swing of the golf club, the flourishing follow-through of the bowling delivery. Spend approximately two minutes in this mode.

b. **Lateral left eye shift code.** This activates the storage of auditory memory, what the motion sounds like when performed correctly—the thud of the "sweet spot" of the racket, bat or clubhead making contact with the ball, the solid clump of the bowling ball hitting the "pocket" and the crash of scattering pins. Spend approximately two minutes in this mode.

c. **Lower left eye shift code.** This keys you into the storage of emotional memory. Use this code to capture all of the emotions and excitement generated by the sports event you are viewing on television—the adrenalin that flows in the golfer as the gallery around the green hushes as he prepares to stroke a key putt, that feeling of confidence and self-efficacy and the self-talk he is using—"I'm consistent, I'm in control, I know I can do it at will!"—as he enters the tenth frame needing only one more strike to clinch the match. Spend approximately two minutes in this mode.

d. **Lower right eye shift code.** This activates the storage of kinesthetic memory; the sensation of movement and motion associated with action on your television screen—what it feels like in terms of body motion, feeling and touch to execute a perfect nine-iron approach shot that drops the ball four feet from the pin.

e. **Central focus eye shift code.** This blends and activates in synchrony all of the senses associated with the movement. Use this central eye focus for the remainder of your television input.

3. If you are watching intensive, continuous action, such as a tennis tournament where play is virtually non-stop, our recommendation is that your coding session extend no longer than 20 minutes. Beyond this, your attention span will begin to waver. On the other hand, if you are watching a sporting event where the action is more spasmodic, such as the telecast of a golf tournament, you could extend your input programming to an hour or more, concentrating on specific aspects of the game you particularly want to sharpen, such as pitch shots or putting.

4. After you have completed your coding session, turn off the television, relax in your chair, and with your eyes closed use the upper left eye shift to key into the color BLUE. Learn to use this eye-shift code and color as a stop-and-start code. Just as you used it to initiate your coding session, you also use it to complete it. Blue also provides a respite and a sealant. When you close your eyes after watching television intensively at one focal point, you will experience an after-image as the electrical activity in the mind continues to resonate at its frequency level. Flooding the mind with the color blue helps calm this down and gets you ready for the next stage in the program—the instant replay.

5. Immediately after your television coding session—having allowed the color BLUE to calm down the after-images—relax in your chair with your eyes closed, key once more into the upper left eye-shift code, and "replay" the mental video tape you have created, recalling as much detail of the action as possible.

Select from this raw, "unedited" tape two or three particular motions that you would like to incorporate into your own game—the ones you concentrated on while watching the television program. Let's say there was a particular golf swing that impressed you. Having isolated this swing on your mental tape, you practice it as follows:

a. With your eyes closed, key into the **upper left eye-shift code** and recall the color BLUE.

b. **Upper left eye shift code.** Mentally replay the entire stroke or movement from an *external* (as you saw it on the screen) visual perspective in as much precise visual detail as possible. Replay this 10 times.

c. **Upper left eye shift code.** Repeat this from an *internal* perspective (as though you were actually inside the athlete you saw on the screen, performing the motion yourself). Replay this 10 times.

d. **Lateral left eye shift code.** From an *external* perspective mentally replay the sounds associated with the motion. Replay this 10 times.

e. **Lateral left eye shift code.** Repeat this from an *internal* perspective. Replay this 10 times.

f. **Lower left eye shift code.** From an external perspective replay, enlarge and magnify all of the positive emotional sensations you felt while watching the action on television.

g. **Lower left eye shift code.** Repeat this from an internal perspective.

h. **Lower right eye shift code.** From an external perspective replay the complete sensation of movement and motion associated with your mental tape sequence, gaining a sense of a grooved fluid motion and the "feel" associated with the correct execution of the motion. (Note: When activating this kinesthetic memory, it is helpful to replay your mental tape in slow motion, just like the instant replays on television. This helps you build a slow, relaxed tempo into your game—a sense of being hurried, of forcing your shots, is the last thing you need!). Replay this 10 times.

i. **Lower right eye shift code.** Repeat this from an internal perspective. Replay this 10 times.

j. **Central focus eye shift code.** From an external perspective mentally replay the action blending all of the senses. Replay this 10 times.

k. **Central focus eye shift code.** Repeat this from an internal perspective. Replay this 10 times.

Conclusion

a. **Upper left eye shift code.** Slowly reverse the colors working from blue to red, associating each color with its specific body zone. Complement each association with a **lower right eye shift code.**

b. **Central focus eye shift code.** Slowly open the eyes and shake out the arms and legs. At this point you will be relaxed, vitalized and clear minded.

Daily Exercises

Just as you practice your game physically, you can practice it mentally with the replay technique just described. And you can do it without leaving home and in a short period of time. However, we do urge you to *give it time*. Don't rush out immediately after your television input session to see if it works.

Instead, try to spend a week at this mental practice before you next play. Repeat the mental replay exercises (beginning with your standard relaxation/concentration color activation) *once a day*. Ideally, if you watch and input a television sports event on a Sunday, the following Saturday would be a good time to schedule your next game.

Video feedback on a home television screen played an important behind-the-scenes role in a major sports story of

THE INSIDE-OUT TEST

As part of your television program coding, you are asked to replay sports motions mentally from both an external perspective (as you actually saw the motion performed on the screen) and from an internal perspective (as though you were actually inside the athlete you saw on the screen). Because individuals have different thought processes, you may find one of these perspectives more difficult to achieve than the other.

For example, if you are a person who tends to view things objectively—from the right side of the brain—you are likely to be more facile at viewing a sports motion from the internal perspective. Conversely, if you are an objective thinker, you probably will be more adept at viewing a sports motion from the external perspective—left side of the brain. Knowing whether you are an external or internal thinker provides a subtle indicator of dominant sensory traits. For example, if the external perspective comes easily to you, the use of the upper right eye-shift code will be a particularly useful tool in enabling you to construct images. If you are more at home with the internal perspective, the lower right eye-shift code usually will prove to be a valuable tool, enabling you to have a highly-developed sense of feel and touch.

To test your dominant trait—internal vs. external—try this simple test:

IMAGINE YOUR FACE AS THE FACE OF A CLOCK AND USE A FINGER TO TOUCH THE 3 O'CLOCK POSITION

Conclusions:

If you indicated your right cheek you are an internal thinker.

If you indicated your left cheek, you are an external thinker.

1980. That was the season that Kansas City Royals' third base-man, George Brett, was engaged in his much-publicized pursuit of a .400 batting average. Whenever Brett felt that he was slipping out of his hitting "groove," losing his touch at the plate, he would go into the basement of his home and replay over and over on his video machine a segment of tape from one of his more notable single-game hitting performances. This was a play-off contest against the New York Yankees when, in front of the Yankee Stadium home crowd, Brett slugged three home runs.

By watching these video-tape replays of his most concen-trated performance under the pressure of intense competition, Brett was able to activate and reinforce the hot-streak "blue-prints" of consistent motion and the associated emotions stored in his brain. Without realizing it, the Royals hitter was utilizing a type of SyberVision training.

George Brett attributes his successful 1980 major-league campaign to the sound fundamentals taught him by his batting coach and to the reinforcement of those fundamentals on his home video tapes. We believe that by using the SyberVision program, George Brett could have been even more consistent because it would have given him a systematic understanding and discipline by which he could have had even greater control of the hot streak or "SyberVision phenomenon."

If you own a video machine (industry forecasters predict that these units eventually will become as commonplace as color television sets, with 20 million video units expected to be in American homes by 1985) you have the opportunity to follow George Brett's example and make your television input even more effective. By taping segments of televised sports action that you wish to incorporate into your own game you will be able to build a library of source tapes to supplement and rein-force the "mental" tapes you make during your television coding sessions. (In production as this book was going to press

Typical home video equipment: video camera and video recorder (PHOTO
COURTESY OF CENTER VIDEO CENTER, CHICAGO)

are special SyberVision Muscle Memory Programming Video Tapes. Available for various sports, these tapes take the fundamental motions and break them down into segments designed to activate the sensory storage areas of the brain. They are available from Professional Development Associates, Inc., 2450 Washington Avenue, Suite 220, San Leandro, California 94577.)

7

Getting the Most out of Professional Instruction

It is neither the design of SyberVision nor the intent of this book to attempt to equip you with the fundamentals of your chosen sport. Our working assumption is that you already have a knowledge—if not a mastery—of the basics of your sport and are playing at least at the five percent consistency level (five well-executed movements out of every 100 attempts).

If you are a golfer, you have already chosen a grip that feels right for you—be it the Vardon, the interlocking or even the baseball grip—and you have a working knowledge of the steps involved in setting up to address the ball. Similarly, tennis players will have a basic understanding of grip variations as well as of such basics as the execution of the correct ball toss and wrist action for effective serves. Certainly, in any sport you will find excellent basic instructional guides to help you master these fundamentals.

If you are like most weekend athletes who take up a sport, you probably got started by borrowing, renting or buying some equipment and simply going out to play, to have fun. As you found that you enjoyed that particular sport, you probably began to read some basic books about it, solicited more experienced players for advice and maybe even took a few lessons. Gradually, your performance started to improve and eventually you reached the plateau that we refer to as "the five-percent consistency level." At this point, you found that your game was producing occasional flashes of brilliance—such as those immensely satisfying, but unfortunately all-too-rare occasions on the golf course when you smash a fairway wood 200 yards and drop it on the green. Mostly, though, your game seemed to be characterized by frustrating inconsistency, such as when you completely fluff that fairway wood shot and the ball rolls an embarrassing 20 yards ahead—no better than you managed to do on Day One when you first took up the sport.

This is the point when the weekend athlete often decides it is time to seek some professional instruction. We heartily endorse this. But at the same time we also wish to offer some guidelines to help you acquire the kind of instruction that is most likely to be fruitful. And we will show you how to use Syber-Vision techniques to get the maximum benefit from instruction.

Since the essence of SyberVision is to create instinctive motion as a conditioned reflex, it is important that when you receive instruction it is keyed into the RIGHT cerebral hemisphere. As you will recall, it is the right side of the brain, activated in the SyberVision program by the color BLUE, that handles the processing of sensory information relating to sight, sound, touch and emotional memory. It is important, therefore, to find a teaching pro who is sensitive toward the visual side of the game, one who emphasizes sensory instruction, one who offers his own form as a model.

One of the authors recalls a bitter experience during high-school years when he took some golf lessons at a driving range. The resident teaching pro explained the role of the hands, arms, shoulders and hips and described in confusing detail all of the component parts of the swing and the principles that govern it. When his student got set to hit the ball he was so tense, thinking about all of these things to do, that he could barely move the club. Not once did that instructor say, "Watch how I do it, and then you try to imitate what I do."

Look for a pro who teaches by using himself as a model. And look for one who accentuates the positive. Prevalent among athletic instructors is the tendency to tear apart a student's game in an effort to weed out the flaws. We strongly believe this to be a fallacious approach to teaching because by emphasizing what the student is doing wrong the teacher reinforces negative cycling and at the same time creates tension. Some instructors even offer video analysis of a student's game, and the student will sit watching himself perform on the video screen as the pro tears his game apart. This, in fact, has a double negative impact. It creates a tremendous psychological barrier of inferiority and it saturates the student with visual input of his own imperfect sports movements to such an extent that he probably will have difficulty in sloughing them off. In effect, this practice of analyzing negatives often turns out to be counter-productive and certainly works negatively against the principles of SyberVision training.

It pays to search out an instructor who is prepared to review your game and recognize the five-percent consistency level— as one of those 20 practice tennis serves you deliver is well executed. This is the teaching pro who says, "Okay, here's what you are doing right. Your brain already knows how to do it correctly, so let's see how we can set about activating it." This kind of approach to athletic instruction also serves to give you a taste of success and imbues you psychologically with that extra dimension of fulfillment.

When you code sports instruction into your brain, there are two basic pitfalls to avoid: 1. over-analysis; 2. reinforcement of imperfect motions. If you fall into the trap of regarding an athletic movement in terms of its component parts—in a golf swing, the cocking of the wrists, the straightness of the leading arm, the positioning of the elbow—you can become a victim of that "paralysis by analysis" that we mentioned earlier. It happens when you inappropriately apply the left side of the brain—the cerebral hemisphere that deals with rational and logical thought processes and with analytical functions—to the task of creating a desired athletic motion that should be a reflexive function of the right side of the brain. In terms of SyberVision training, it means you are activating the conditioning color GREEN when you should be activating the conditioning color BLUE.

A second problem occurs when you activate the appropriate side of the brain but flood it with inappropriate input—such as when a teaching professional insists upon concentrating on your mistakes instead of emphasizing those movements you are executing correctly. This problem also can occur when you play with a partner whose game is inferior to your own and you unconsciously key into faulty elements of that person's game.

Even a seasoned pro can fall victim to these phenomena. Let's take a classic example of an athlete who has spent many years in competition on the professional tour and who has enjoyed some measure of success. He decides that the time has come to quit the hassle, pressure and constant travel of the pro tour and take a comfortable job as resident teaching pro at a local club. He still enters the occasional tournament, only to find that he is no longer able to be competitive. His game seems to have fallen off, despite the fact that he maintains the same level of practice that he adhered to while on tour, and despite being involved with the game on a fundamental level almost daily.

That instructor has fallen victim to the "teaching syndrome" that is not uncommon among teaching professionals (although, often, they may be at a loss to explain it). Two things happen. First, when an individual attempts to teach an athletic movement to someone else, it forces the teacher to approach the instinctive movements of that sport at an analytical level. When a pro begins to analyze a motion that he has for years performed unthinkingly as a conditioned reflex, he opens up his game to the conscious mind; he calls upon the cognitive powers of the left cerebral hemisphere.

Second, that teacher becomes so concentrated on trying to analyze what the student is doing wrong that he makes himself susceptible to the visual input of that imperfect motion. This input begins to resonate at the frequency level at which is stored his own performance blueprints. This is like introducing a mongrel strain into a pedigree bloodline. As a result, when he goes out to play he is bombarded with this visual input of imperfection which starts to interfere with the skills which he once produced as a conditioned reflex. As his game begins to deteriorate, he starts to analyze his own motions—motions which he previously had performed automatically—and he becomes caught up in a vicious cycle.

Conscious and unconscious imitation also is a factor to take into account when playing with partners or against opponents at various skill levels. You probably have observed that when you play with an individual whose skills are at a superior level to your own invariably your own play improves. Conversely, when your playing partner has skills that are inferior to your own, your own game seems to deteriorate.

In choosing playing partners, we recommend an approach that we call the "one-third formula." With this system, approximately one-third of your playing time should be with partners or against opponents who are more skilled than yourself. If you key into your visual sensory memory using an upper left eye-shift you will be able to "rob" this person of some of his or her superior form. We are not suggesting that you consciously attempt to imitate your opponent. Simply open up your mind to receive input. This enables your sensory frequencies to be saturated by your opponent's superior form and it will help you improve your own game.

For the second one-third of your partners or opponents choose athletes who are about on a par with yourself. This provides a challenge and helps you build a competitive edge. For this type of opponent, it is important to concentrate on the psychological side of the game—since you do not want to pick up this person's skills, they being no further advanced than your own. Use the lower left eye-shift code to activate emotional input—all of the feelings associated with striving to best an opponent with whom you are equally matched.

For the remaining one-third of your playing time, choose opponents whose game is at a lesser level than your own. In these situations, it is important to again key into emotional sensory input by using the lower left eye-shift code. The object is to use these winning situations to improve your own confidence level and build a memory bank of all the positive emotions and feelings associated with success. With this type of opponent you turn off visual input. In tennis, for example, you would attempt to concentrate on the ball coming over the net, mentally dissolving your opponent as if he or she did not exist.

TECHNIQUES FOR SPORTS INSTRUCTION

Assuming you have located an instructor who uses a visual approach to teaching and who believes in reinforcing and building upon your existing level of consistency, rather than dwelling on the flaws in your technique, it then becomes a simple matter of applying SyberVision techniques you already have mastered to create an environment for maximum learning. (Incidentally, don't overlook group lessons—providing the instructor offers himself or herself as a practical teaching model—as an inexpensive means of obtaining instruction.) Once you have decided to take professional instruction, the object is to use SyberVision relaxation and concentration techniques to make you more receptive to it and to use the SyberVision replay technique (the same system you use following input from television) to practice and reinforce that instruction mentally.

1. **Preparation.** Before heading out to take a lesson, complete the Syber-Relaxation and Syber-Concentration exercises described in chapters Four and Five. By this time, you probably will be more than six to eight weeks into the program and will have progressed to the abbreviated Advanced Exercise (see page 69) where, as a daily routine, you simply cue into activating colors with an upper left eye-shift code and progress from the color red to the color violet for each of the six Syber Zones. Once weekly you will be completing the full relaxation/concentration exercise.

If you are taking one lesson a week, try to schedule it on the same day you have set aside for your weekly session with the full-blown relaxation-concentration exercise. If you cannot do this, schedule your daily SyberVision relaxation/concentration exercise—even the abbreviated version—to precede as closely as possible your sports lesson. By so doing, you will find that you will be tremendously relaxed and that your powers of concentration will be at the peak of effectiveness, with the right side of the brain activated and ready to accept visual input. The nine men and seven women of the Stanford University tennis teams who took SyberVision training reported that going through their relaxation and concentration exercises before going out onto the practice court made them more relaxed, produced a more fluid movement and enhanced the retention of the motions they performed.

2. **During instruction.** When you arrive for your lesson, just

before instruction begins take a minute or two to run through the color codes as follows:

a. **Upper left eye-shift code,** cue into the activating color RED.

b. Repeat for the color ORANGE.

c. Repeat for the color YELLOW.

d. Repeat for the color GREEN.

e. Repeat for the color BLUE.

When you reach the color BLUE, the conditioning color for the right cerebral hemisphere, pinpoint that color in the center of the had and slowly allow it to expand until you feel that your entire head, from the top of the scalp to the base of the neck, is flooded with blue. This entire exercise takes only a few minutes, but it results in the activation and sharpening of the visual senses. Your brain now is primed to store sensory input that will help maximize the benefits of your lesson.

Note: We have stressed repeatedly in this chapter the value of visually-oriented instruction and the importance of stressing positives—enlarging upon your existing five percent level of consistency. In so doing, our intention is not to discredit the concept of negative feedback as a teaching tool. On the contrary, we believe that it has an important function both in sports teaching and in sports practice.

Negative feedback is useful in reviewing, adjusting and practicing the fundamentals of a sport. Use it at the beginning of a lesson to review the non-sensory elements of your game. For example, a golf pro, prior to demonstrating the smooth, effortless flow of the swing, may take you aside to review the basics of your style. He may suggest adjustments in your grip, set-up or, perhaps, provide guidelines for re-positioning the placement of the feet as you play shorter irons. This is a relevant and effective use of negative feedback inasmuch as it deals with cognitive rather than sensory input.

In terms of SyberVision programming, this simply means that you prepare to receive this cognitive instruction by activating your left cerebral hemisphere. Accomplish this simply by keying into the color GREEN using the upper left eye-shift code. When completing your relaxation/concentration exercise prior to instruction, stop at the color GREEN, use this mode for cognitive input relating to fundamentals, and then continue into the BLUE mode to code in sensory blueprints of the visual segment of the teaching session.

Similarly, when you practice, it is helpful to activate the GREEN color cue to review your fundamentals before moving into the BLUE mode to activate sensory memory stored in the right side of the brain. It is okay even to practice a sports motion in the green mode if you are seeking an analytical perspective on the dynamics of the motion, e.g. trying to adjust your basic technique for the backswing at golf or for your backhand at tennis. However, once you have nailed down this fundamental adjustment, be sure to move into the sensory blue mode for "blueprinting" that motion and establishing it as a conditioned response.

3. **Following instruction.** After you have completed your lesson, use the upper left eye-shift code to once again flood the mind with the color BLUE. Remember, this color is also a stop-and-start code that provides a respite for the optic nerves and that also serves as a sealant to help "fix" the visual input you have just coded in.

When you arrive home, replay and review in your mind the mental tape you created during the lesson. Select the particular segments you wish to reinforce and play them over and over on a daily basis from each of the sensory perspectives—visual, emotional, auditory, kinesthetic—just as you did with the mental tape you created while watching televised sports, as described in the previous chapter.

Gradually, with each new input—from television, from sports lessons, from superior-skilled opponents—you are enlarging your sensory memory bank. As a result, the five-percent consistency level is beginning to expand and you will find yourself playing better and winning more often. If in selecting opponents and playing partners you are using the one-third formula we suggest, you are finding that the composition of those thirds is ever-changing. Some of those individuals who were in the top one-third category have slipped into the middle one-third grouping as you find yourself winning against them more often than you lose. You find yourself looking for even better players to fill in the top one-third. And so it goes. It means that SyberVision is at work, improving your game.

8

Your Pre-Competition
Sensory Rehearsal

Often, there is one big day for sports in the weekly routine of
the average casual athlete. If you are a bowler, it may be the
evening that you play in league competition. If you are a golfer,
it may be Saturday morning, when the alarm goes off in the
pre-dawn hours to awaken you for a weekly rendezvous on the
first tee. If you are a tennis player, it may be Sunday afternoon
when, after a week of practice at an indoor court, you pit your
skills head-on with a really tough opponent.

The intent of this chapter is to help you get yourself ready for
that big game or match. If you have followed the programs
outlined in the preceding chapters, you already have done much
of the groundwork. You will have learned how to use Syber-
Vision coding techniques to become more relaxed, to sharpen
your powers of concentration. You will have applied these same
techniques to transform televised sports events into unique
vehicles for learning, as well as to make sports instruction more
effective. And you will have learned to use the SyberVision
process to "borrow" skills from superior opponents while using
lesser- or equally-skilled playing partners as a source of psychological strength.

Probably by now you feel primed to play, ready to put Syber-Vision techniques to work in that important game or match. Well, you are—almost! However, before you go out to keep your weekly golf, tennis or bowling date, there is one more important preparatory step that can make your SyberVision training even more effective. You are going to stage a pre-competition rehearsal!

Just as in show business, before you take your act on the road you are going to have a dress rehearsal. As in the theater, this will be a full-stage production of the real thing. However, it won't happen on the golf course, the bowling lane or the tennis court. It will be staged in your own mind. You will create in your mind in as much sensory detail as possible exactly the way you desire to perform in the big game (within the limits of your own capabilities, of course—you can't expect to transform yourself overnight into a sports superstar). In effect, you will be creating sensory goals for yourself. You will be coding into that magnificent mental computer of yours a desired future per-formance—so that when you go out to play you can activate that stored memory (not forcing it, but simply allowing it to happen as you prelived it).

In staging your sensory pre-competition rehearsal, timing is crucial. It is important to schedule your rehearsal exercise *no later than 24 hours* prior to competition and *no earlier than 48 hours* prior to an upcoming game. This moratorium allows time for sensory input to settle and take root in the brain. Were you to rehearse within 24 hours of competition, your input would be too recent and would have a negative effect on your game. You would find yourself forcing activation of that stored memory, and this creates tension. The idea when you go out to play is to forget that rehearsal and let your pre-lived experience bring itself to the surface. Tell yourself, "Okay, I know it's in there and I am going out to play as well as I can and allow the right side of my brain to express itself. And if that doesn't happen, it's okay. If I should fluff a shot, I'm not going to get mad. My body is an instrument of my brain. I have a working relationship with it and I am going to relax and enjoy myself while it does the work."

This seems an appropriate point to offer a reminder not to expect your SyberVision training program to produce instant success. SyberVision is a discipline, a long-term building process that will be reflected in the *gradual* improvement of your abilities at a particular sport as you steadily expand your level of consistency. Be patient and allow that improvement to occur naturally; do not deliberately try to force or hurry the program. Remember, your right cerebral hemisphere already has a blueprint of those flawless sports motions; give yourself time to develop a relationship between your body and your brain.

PRE-COMPETITION REHEARSAL CODING

Having selected an appropriate time for rehearsal—you should spend at least an hour at it—within the 24-48-hour time frame, proceed as follows:

1. Settle yourself into your SyberVision quiet spot—comfortably stretched out in chair or on couch, free from any noise or distractions, attired in loose-fitting clothing with any weighty or binding objects such as belt, watch and glasses removed.

2. Complete the Syber-Relaxation/Syber-Concentration exercise at whatever level you have progressed to. Probably, by now, you have reached the Advanced Exercise, which is simply a matter of recalling, with an upper left eye-shift code, the activating colors for each of the body zones—RED, ORANGE, YELLOW, GREEN, BLUE, VIOLET.

3. Cue into the color GREEN, the activating color for the left cerebral hemisphere. The object of this part of the rehearsal is

to code into the cognitive or analytical side of the brain your pre-game strategy. For example, in golf, a sport in which week-end athletes typically have fixed habits, playing week after week on a course that is as familiar as a well-worn golf glove, this part of the rehearsal should be used to establish a hole-by-hole strategy for playing that course. Decide where you want each tee shot to land, how you will play each approach shot; set your strategies for dealing with specific problems posed by the architecture of the course, such as narrow fairways, tricky dog legs, water hazards, bunkers and sand traps, critical pin placements; work out the holes where you plan to "lay up" and those where you intend to "go for the flag." In essence, you are programming into your mental computer a strategic scenario for your upcoming venture onto the local links.

In tennis this tactical planning might be to decide whether your game plan will be to attack aggressively at the net or to play back at the baseline, whether you will emphasize playing the sidelines or the center line. Also use this green-state strategic rehearsal to analyze an opponent's strengths and weaknesses and to set up tactics to neutralize those strengths and exploit those weaknesses. In bowling, you might use this tactical rehearsal session to review your set-up and approach and to determine whether you will be spot bowling or pin bowling. In rehearsing for an upcoming bowling-league game, you would set up performance goals, programming into your mental computer the specifics of attaining a desired score—by how many points you plan to exceed your average, and how you will accomplish it, frame-by-frame.

Goal setting is an important part of strategic rehearsal. We recommend that you set your goal at improving your most recent typical performance by 50 percent. For example, if your bowling average is 120, set your sights when rehearsing strategy on bowling at 180 in your upcoming game. In golf, if you typically shoot at around 100, set your strategy for a round of

85—50 percent of the difference between your past performance and par.

In tennis, program this 50-percent improvement factor into your left cerebral hemisphere by analyzing your last performance against an upcoming opponent and set the goal of improving on the spread of sets. If on your last outing you struggled to win in extra sets, program for your upcoming time a decisive 6-3, 6-3 victory.

In skiing, map out your strategy for tackling a specific run—how you will handle the terrain, how you will negotiate moguls, how you will cut the edges of the skis. In sports such as football and basketball, where every member of the team has specific responsibilities, use this green-state strategy session to rehearse how you will set up to handle your individual assignment in various play patterns. In baseball, as in bowling, the object would be to use this green-state tactical rehearsal to improve a batting average in a given performance by 50 percent—set the goal of getting, say, three hits in five appearances at the plate.

4. Reverting to our theatrical analogy, you now have your strategy set—all of your lines and cues memorized, all of your stage directions down pat. You now need to give your natural ability a chance to assert itself. For this, you need a warm-up, borrowing from performance memory tucked away in your mental storehouse. In effect, this stage of the rehearsal is a mental practice session designed to activate that stored sensory memory before applying it, stroke-by-stroke, play-by-play as you pre-live in your mind that upcoming game. This helps you mentally "groove" your game as you experience the fluidity of motion and all of the feelings and emotions associated with it through activation of all of the senses.

For this stage of the rehearsal, cue into the color BLUE, the conditioning color for activating sensory input into the right cerebral hemisphere. Replay in your mind a mental tape of a recent performance or recent training session. This could also be a memory blueprint you created from television (and have since edited and mentally "practiced" every day) or a mental tape created from a sports lesson. For golf, this warm-up tape will usually be the motion of your basic swing; in tennis, the forehand, backhand and serve; in bowling, the entire motion of approach and delivery—and so on.

Play this warm-up tape five times from each sensory perspective, cueing yourself in with the appropriate eye codes. For example, replay your basic golf swing five times from the visual sensory perspective (upper left eye-shift code) to capture how that swing looks; five times from the auditory perspective (lateral left eye-shift code) to accentuate the sound of that swing; five times from the emotional perspective (lower left eye-shift code) to pick up on the emotions associated with that successful swing, capturing, even as you set up, the feeling of your body and mind being linked as one and intensifying that hunger to win—also use this access to the emotional sensory storage compartment of the right-side brain to diffuse the effects of negative performance, telling yourself that you plan to forget about and put behind you any mistakes you might make; five times from the kinesthetic perspective (lower right eye-shift code) to focus upon how that well-executed swing feels; and, finally, five times from the total sensory perspective (central focus eye-shift code) to blend and harmonize all of the senses.

5. You now have the strategy set and the motor system activated. You have keyed into both sides of the brain and have primed each to do its specific job—analytical and sensory. The next step is to get both sides to work in harmony, to establish a working relationship between your mind and your body. This is where you harness the sixth Syber Zone, the corpus callosum, a body of connecting fiber that acts as a link between the functions of each cerebral hemisphere. This is activated by the conditioning color VIOLET, as follows:

a. **Upper left eye-shift code.** Recall the color VIOLET, the conditioning color for access to the corpus callosum. Picture the corpus callosum as a bridge linking the left and right sides of the brain. Across the bridge runs an electric conduit filled with wires and circuitry. This provides the free exchange of communication and electrical energy between the two cerebral hemispheres.

b. **Lower right eye-shift code.** Sense the corpus callosum bridging both sides of the brain.

c. **Upper right eye-shift code.** Beam the color VIOLET to the corpus callosum region of the brain.

d. **Lower right eye-shift code.** Sense the clarity of mind and sharpening of the senses that accompanies access into this connecting area of the brain. Sense a feeling of wholeness, of joining, as both sides of the brain work in synchrony.

e. **Upper right eye-shift code.** This code provides access into the area of your brain that deals with constructed visual images, for putting things together that are not reality—such as the red-winged chimpanzee with a giraffe's neck in our earlier exercise. It is the code you use for preliving an upcoming sports event. It is the signal for beginning your step-by-step pre-competition rehearsal.

f. **Central focus eye-shift code.** Use this central focus to activate a total sensory experience. If you are a golfer, prelive the playing of those 18 holes in as much sensory detail as possible. As you approach the first tee, feel that strong desire—almost a hunger—to win; experience this sensation of invincibility through every pore and fiber of your body. Then picture yourself standing on the first tee with the collar of your windcheater turned up against the early-morning chill. Feel the supple leather of your golf glove as you wriggle your fingers into it, the bite of your spikes into the turf as you set up to address the ball. Follow the damp track your ball makes in the dew on the green as it rolls toward the hole. Feel the

Preliving your sports victory

club in your hand, hear the solid smack of contact with the ball. Feel the emotional strength and confidence you experience as you perform successfully. Sense yourself moving fluidly through the motions of your swing. Hear the complimentary reactions of your playing companions to your superb shot-making. Write an imaginary newspaper article that details your fine performance—"John Smith Shoots a Sparkling 85!"

Whatever your sport, the object is to create as much input as possible using all of the senses. If you are a skier, you want to feel the edges of your skis cutting into fine powder snow, sense the flexing of the knees, the implanting of the poles, feel the breeze against your face, hear the rush of air past your flying body—even gain a sense of the ski clothes you'll wear, such as goggles, hat and gloves.

Take your time as you pre-live that upcoming performance, even to the extent of slowing down the action to a kind of slow motion. Above all, make it an exhilarating experience.

g. **Upper left eye-shift code.** Recall from memory the color VIOLET to signal to the brain the end of the pre-competition coding.

Conclusion

h. **Upper left eye-shift code.** Slowly reverse the colors working down from VIOLET to RED, associating each color with its specific body zone. Complement each association with a **lower right eye-shift code.**

i. **Central focus eye-shift code.** Slowly open the eyes and shake out the arms and legs. At this point you will be relaxed, vitalized and clear-minded.

At this point, your philosophy should be: "Now my brain knows exactly how to perform because that performance already has been coded in. The difficult part has been done. My neurological computer has been programmed and 24 hours from now, when I go out to play, all I need do is to key in the variables and hit the button to start the computer running.''

The important consideration when you arrive at the golf course, tennis court, bowling lane, etc., is not to force yourself to live up to your expectations. Do *not* deliberately set out to re-enact the performance you have rehearsed mentally. Simply let it happen. Play with confidence and as instinctively as possible without concerning yourself with fundamentals. Let both sides of your brain work in harmony and regard your body as an instrument of whatever they dictate.

9

Putting SyberVision to Work on Your Game

So now you are ready to play. You've learned how to relax and how to concentrate. Modeling from performances of professional or top amateur players you watch on television, from sports instructors and from opponents with superior skills, you have been building and enlarging a positive memory bank of the correct motion for your sport from every sensory perspective. You know how that motion looks, feels and sounds, and you have keyed into sensory memory all of the emotions and feelings associated with it. You have even gone one step further. You have actually rehearsed, in exquisite sensory detail, the very match you now are going to play.

Now you find yourself standing on that first tee looking out at the fairway, or slipping out of your warm-up suit at the tennis court, or being introduced to players on the opposing team for your bowling-league tournament. What comes next?

Really, it's quite simple, because you already have done the difficult part. You already have played that match neurologically. Now it is simply a matter of going out to relive it. Let yourself experience that sense of *deja vu*.

Begin by recalling, with an upper left eye-shift code, the

activating color for each of the body zones—RED, ORANGE, YELLOW, GREEN, VIOLET—just as you did prior to your rehearsal. Then, once you have cued into the color VIOLET, go out and merely try to keep the ball in play. Don't think at all about fundamentals; instead, concentrate your thoughts on strategy. Because everything else has been conditioned and that VIOLET cue is set to activate whatever you did in your rehearsal. It's a start-up code for that program you put into your mind.

You also must be willing to accept that inevitably you will make some bad plays. Be ready to put any mistakes behind you without dwelling on them or allowing them to upset or frustrate you. This does not mean that you must accept a negative performance or be complacent about your miscues. It also is important to maintain an aggressive edge. Keep your game sharp by keying into positive memory. Use the upper left eye-shift code to key into those occasions when you performed well and to experience the sensory memory of those past successes. In golf, for example, where you may play frequently on one particular course, there are certain holes that are your bane. It seems that you always play these holes badly. This, too, becomes a conditioned response—in this instance, an undesirable one—because even though there may have been occasions when you executed well on these particular holes, it is the negative that overwhelms your memory. The negative waves scramble your sensory frequency and result in a jerky, impure motion. And this, in turn, creates tension. Again, overcome negative response by activating the memory of superior play.

Learn to regard SyberVision as a real working tool, a constant playing companion. At any time during play feel free to use any of the eye-shift codes to draw from sensory memory. Perhaps in a tennis match your serve is not working as well as you would wish. As you stand on the baseline ready to deliver your serve this would be an appropriate time to draw from your reservoir of stored sensory memory.

First, use the upper left eye-shift code to "see" that well-executed serve. Then switch to the lower right eye-shift code to capture the feeling of muscle motion and body movement associated with a smooth, flowing, one-piece delivery. Next, use the lateral left eye-shift code to key into the sound of that perfect serve, the swish of the racket and the twang of the ball hitting solidly against its taut strings. Finally, key into the lower-left eye-shift code to draw psychological strength from the emotional memories associated with superior serves you have executed in the past, building confidence and certainty and dissolving doubt and fear.

Similarly, as you play, you can call upon your Syber-Relaxation technique to melt away tension in any area of the body simply by recalling the activating color cue. If, for example, you are experiencing tension in your hands and arms, you would recall the color ORANGE (conditioning color for the upper torso), project that color into the hands and arms using an upper right eye-shift code and then, with a lower right eye-shift code, focus on sensing the surge of revitalizing oxygenation of the muscle tissue and the resultant release of tension —just as you do in your daily and weekly sessions.

Also, as you play, you will want to use the SyberVision technique to capture for future reference those well-executed shots or strokes that you make. After you complete a shot, stroke or a series of motions that feels good and achieves the desired result, simply footnote it for retention and replay it through all the sensory modes. Using an upper left eye-shift code, replay the shot visually, gaining a real sense of what it looked like. Using the lateral left eye-shift code, relive the sounds associated with that fine play. Using the lower right eye-shift code, feel the shot from the kinesthetic perspective. Using the lower left eye-shift code, experience all of the positive and satisfying emotional aspects of your successful play-making. Replay the motion once from each eye-shift pattern. It takes but a moment and strongly reinforces this motion in the memory, earmarking it for attention in the next stage of your SyberVision program, post-competition mental editing (see Chapter 11).

During competition, also use the lower left eye-shift code to engage in confidence-bolstering self-talk—"I am consistent! I can do it because I already know how to do it. I've already done it successfully." Employ this self-talk also for goal-setting, to provide the right cerebral hemisphere with objectives (but *never* fundamentals) . . . "I want this shot on the back of the green . . . I'm going to ace this serve . . . I'm going to make my second consecutive strike."

However, any time a goal is not achieved, don't get down on yourself, because in punishing yourself you also are shutting off memory flow. Try to play as naturally as possible and let your game happen. Remember, you already have rehearsed it. (Nonetheless this rehearsal should not be deliberately recalled. Blank out of your mind the fact that you have programmed your game in rehearsal. Simply activating the color VIOLET as a cue is sufficient to activate that program you coded into your mind. You hit the button and let your automatic pilot take over.)

Again, we would stress that you should not expect Syber-Vision training to transform a weekend athlete into a sports superstar. It is, however, a mental discipline that can help accelerate learning and help you acquire skills much faster—providing you give it time to take root. Don't be disappointed if you don't show a marked improvement the first two or three times you play competitively. It may have taken years to form those bad habits you are trying to break. It takes time to change those habits and make the SyberVision learning process a dominant factor.

One of the greatest inhibitors during competition is tension. Often, this results from placing too much importance on competition—viewing it as a make-or-break, do-or-die event. Certainly, there is important self-esteem and satisfaction to be derived from playing well and winning. But let's face it, in the case of most weekend athletes, who is really going to care about the result after the game is over? Compounding this tension is the fear of failure, particularly the fear of embarrassment of performing poorly in front of others.

Let's examine a typical tension-filled situation for a casual athlete. It's early Saturday morning and the golf course is busy with weekend players. You wait with others in your group near the first tee, waiting for the starter to summon you. Several other foursomes also are awaiting their turn and everyone is passing the time watching those groups ahead of them tee off. You know that you'll also have an audience when your turn comes and already you are getting nervous, remembering all of the times you duffed your tee shot, wondering if you will make an embarrassing miscue in front of this audience. Tension and anxiety set in, you begin to choke up. Chances are that by the time you step up to the tee you will be so tense that you *will* flub the shot.

This is where Syber-Demon and Syber-Man enter the picture. These are the SyberVision symbols of negative and positive behavior—the bad guy and the good guy—and we will show you how to put them to work for you to overcome anxiety.

The Syber-Demon is the bad guy, the symbol of self-defeating emotions, thoughts and behavior. It represents anxiety, tension and fear. It stands for all of the negative psychological factors in sport that can erode a performance. It is symbolic of that pounding in the head, that queasy churning in the pit of the stomach, that sense of being rushed, that gnawing feeling that eats away at you like acid. By actually conjuring in your mind a picture of a demon, you are giving a definite form to all of these amorphous negative traits— one that you can deal with firmly. In fact, when we introduce this demon concept to athletes who undergo SyberVision

Syber Demon

training at our California headquarters, we provide a poster with a caricature of the Syber-Demon—a hairy, green bug with black evil eyes and sharp, pointed teeth. Create in your mind your own particular demon—or use the Syber-Demon we have illustrated.

Syber-Man is the anti-demon—our good guy. This is a symbol of strength and confidence, of mental and physical sharpness and quickness. Syber-Man exudes solid aggressiveness, total self-assurance and the sense of a solid foundation. Should you make a bad play, it is Syber-Man who says, "It's okay, I'm not going to get upset about it. It's nobody's fault. My brain knows how to do it . . . we just need to start working together a little more closely." Mentally construct your own strong anti-demon caricature—or use the rendition of Syber-Man used in the SyberVision training program (see illustration). Our armor-clad, sword-wielding warrior bears the head of an eagle with sharp, penetrating eyes to signify sensory acuity. The armor represents your psychological shield that prevents negative thoughts from penetrating your memory banks and interfering with your positive coding.

To experience an effective interplay between the demon and anti-demon, try the following exercises. These techniques are designed for pre-competition conditioning and for use during competition. As you master these techniques, you can begin to control competition anxiety, fear and nervousness and replace those negative, performance-sapping emotions with aggression, confidence, strength and calm assuredness.

EMOTIONAL CONDITIONING EXERCISES

Conditioning Anxiety To The Syber-Demon

The Syber-Demon is the symbol of self-defeating emotions, thoughts and behavior. To associate and condition your self-

SyberMan

defeating competition-related behavior to this symbol, follow these instructions:

1. **Upper left eye-shift code.** Recall from memory the colors RED, ORANGE, YELLOW, GREEN and BLUE.

2. **Upper left eye-shift code.** While in the BLUE right-brain state, open your eyes and focus on the picture of the Syber-Demon (or a drawing of your own particular demon). Focus on the fine detail of the Syber-Demon—its head, eyes, teeth, body, hands, feet, claws, etc.

3. **Lower left eye-shift code.** Recreate from your past experience and relive the negative emotions you would like to associate with the demon, eyes still open.

4. **Lower right eye-shift code.** Recreate the bodily sensations associated with the self-defeating emotions, i.e., pounding heart, butterflies in the pit of the stomach, shakiness, etc.

5. Close your eyes and go to the **Central Focus eye-shift code.** Merge the picture of the Syber-Demon with your emotions and bodily sensations.

Conditioning Strength To Syber-Man

Syber-Man is a symbol of strength and confidence, of mental and physical sharpness and quickness. To associate and condition your inherent strengths, emotions and behavior to this symbol, follow these instructions:

1. **Upper left eye-shift code.** With closed eyes, recall the color BLUE.

2. **Upper left eye-shift code.** Open your eyes and focus on the picture of Syber-Man (or a drawing of a warrior of your own creation). Focus on the fine detail of Syber-Man—the eagle head with sharp beak and penetrating eyes, the strong talons, the sharp sword, the protective armor, etc.

3. **Lower left eye-shift code.** Recreate from your past experience and relive the positive emotions you would like to associate with Syber-Man, eyes still open.

4. **Lower right eye-shift code.** Recreate and relive the bodily sensations associated with the positive emotions, i.e., calmness, a feeling of strength in the stomach area, clarity of mind, a sharp mental focus.

5. Close your eyes and go to the **Central focus eye-shift code.** Merge the picture and characteristics of Syber-Man with your positive emotions and bodily sensations.

Competition Anxiety Control

After you have conditioned the negative and positive emotions respectively to the Syber-Demon and Syber-Man you can begin to control the emotions by controlling the symbols. Put your good guy and bad guy to work for you. When you feel yourself slipping into a state of nervousness, anxiety or self-doubt, you can decode those negative behavioral traits instantly by going through the following exercise:

1. With eyes closed, **upper right eye-shift code.** Engage the Syber-Demon and Syber-Man symbols in an imaginary battle. Imagine in as much vivid detail as possible, Syber-Man totally destroying the Syber-Demon. (Many psychiatrists who deal with the emotional problems of children with catastrophic illness use a similar technique of having patients visualize armies of antibodies engaging and destroying the enemy cells. Steven DeVore used this technique as a child in his successful battle to overcome the crippling effects of polio.)

2. **Upper left eye-shift code.** Recall from memory as vividly as possible the symbol of the victorious Syber-Man.

3. **Lower left eye-shift code.** Sense the emerging strong emotions associated with the victorious symbol.

4. **Upper left eye-shift code.** Visually recall as vividly as possible a picture of yourself.

5. **Upper right eye-shift code.** Merge the picture of yourself into the picture of the Syber-Man symbol.

6. Central focus eye-shift code. Capture the total sensory impact of the emotions and bodily sensations that accompany the merging of yourself with Syber-Man. As a result of previous conditioning, the feelings, emotions and bodily sensations you associated with the Syber-Man symbol will surface.

It will take at least two weeks of conditioning the symbols to the behaviors (30 minutes per day) to condition the desirable responses. After two weeks of this conditioning, you will be ready to use this technique in competition to control anxiety.

One final word about competition: Remember, you are not a robot! You will make mistakes no matter how much you code yourself. By utilizing the SyberVision discipline those mistakes will be much less frequent than under normal training procedures. You also will have the necessary tools to avoid dreadful slumps.

When you make mistakes, be forgiving. Your brain knows how to perform; allow it to work with and for you. If you get mad at yourself you will build up tension and lose concentration, shutting off the lifeline to the brain's rich reservoir of stored muscle memory.

10

SyberTricks and SyberAids

Because SyberVision is a discipline of the mind, the program readily lends itself to mental techniques that can help improve your play. Some of the following suggestions—we call them SyberAids—are designed specifically to enhance the application of your basic SyberVision training program. Others—SyberTricks—are purely sports-specific, mental exercises that you can apply during competition and in practice drills. You may find that these little flights of fantasy can make the difference between sinking a long putt or rolling your ball several feet past the hole, between smacking a line drive for a solid hit and striking out at the plate.

SYBERTRICKS

Tennis

• As an aid to making solid contact with the ball on the "sweet spot" in the center of the racket, imagine that the racket is at least twice its normal size.

• A similar "Alice-in-Wonderland" technique to help you make clean returns is to imagine the ball to be at least twice its normal size. Try to see it large and clear with its spinning seams and fuzzy cover.

• Some tennis players are "net bound"—they fear hitting into the net. As a consequence, the net becomes a psychological as well as a physical barrier and these players seem to hit into it with inordinate frequency. If this is a problem, simply mentally "dissolve" the net and play as though it did not exist.

• If your opponent seems to loom large before you and appears to dominate most of the opposite half of the court, always positioned precisely at the spot you return the ball, you may need more confidence and precision in your shot placement. Try these two mental devices: 1. Enlarge the court on your opponent's side; then, with seemingly larger unoccupied areas of the court to work with, pick your target areas more critically; 2. Shrink your opponent to about half-size— again enlarging your target area and your confidence.

• Another incredible shrinking trick is purely defensive. Mentally scale down your half of the court. Suddenly, you'll find that you are Mr. Speed, reaching and returning well-placed shots that you previously might have conceded as lost points.

• You'll also find that you can achieve more nimble court coverage if you imagine that your shoes are filled with helium. Enhance this illusion by keying into the lower right eye-shift code.

Golf

• Also try the larger-than-life technique on the putting green. You may find yourself sinking more putts if you imagine the hole to be two or three times its normal size.

• Whether you're putting for dough or for show, lining up the shot plays a large part in success. By all means "read" the speed and gradient of the green. Then, as you line up to stroke the ball, try this mental exercise: Picture a line, groove or

SyberTricks: mentally enlarge the ball and bat

channel extending from the position of your ball to the cup and attempt to steer your putt along this imaginary guidepath.

• Sand traps are aptly named. They are a nemesis to many weekend golfers who either understroke or skull the ball and burn several strokes attempting to get out of the sand, or take too much of the ball and send it flying across the green (and often into a twin trap on the other side of the green). When attempting an "explosion" shot from the sand and the ball is not buried too deeply, imagine the open face of your clubhead as a razor blade. Swing easily through the shot visualizing that razor's edge slicing delicately between the underside of the ball and the sand. If properly executed, the ball should pop out of the trap and plop onto the green.

Bowling

• In bowling, the fluid motion of the release and follow-through means that the ball is virtually an extension of the hand. You can heighten this effect by imagining your hand reaching the length of the lane and knocking down the pins with one flourishing sweep.

• Many of these SyberTricks lend themselves to a number of sports. The aid to alignment on the putting green suggested for golfers also can be used effectively by bowlers. Visualize a line, groove or channel extending from the point where your ball will make contact with the lane to its intended target among the pins, and attempt to steer your shot along that imaginary line.

• Another multi-sport exercise that adapts well to bowling is the over-size ball. Imagine a larger-than-life bowling ball scattering the pins for a strike.

Skiing

• Skiers also can benefit from a sensation of floating. Liken your skis to a magic carpet that floats above ground or to hovercraft that skim the surface of the water on a cushion of air. By imagining yourself gliding downhill a few inches above the terrain, your run should be smoother and more in control.

• Before pushing off for a run, picture yourself completing that run in slow motion. This mental exercise, designed to engage all of the senses, has you feeling the wind in your face, hearing the crunch of the skis and the sound of the air rushing past and feeling every twist and turn of your body as you execute all of your reactions to the slope in slow motion.

Baseball

• As a hitter, mentally enlarge the ball so that it is three or four times its normal size. (After his SyberVision training, Oakland A's hitter Mitchell Page went on a slugging spree and noted that the baseball was looking "as big as a grapefruit.") A similar technique for increasing efficiency at the plate is to imagine you are swinging a fatter bat.

• Pitchers can use a similar SyberTrick by enlarging their target—imagining the catcher's mitt to be at least twice its normal size.

• Fielders can sharpen their catching and stopping skills by picturing the ball flying or skipping toward them as being larger than life.

Running

• There are several mental techniques that can help promote the feeling of fleetness of foot: 1. Imagine that you are taking giant-size strides and are thus burning up the ground; 2. Use the helium-filled shoes device we suggest for tennis players to help shake off that "lead feet" feeling. Again, complement this exercise by keying into the lower right eye-shift code. 3. Also capture that lighter-than-air sensation by picturing yourself floating across the ground on a magic carpet or as a hovercraft.

• Most runners are familiar with the "wall effect"—that psychological barrier of fatigue that sets in urging you to quit.

SyberTricks: picture yourself floating across the ground

Mentally dissolve this wall by flooding the mind with the color blue.

Basketball
 • Use the mental enlarging-reducing technique to improve shooting accuracy. Imagine the hoop larger than it actually is and the ball a little smaller than normal size.
 • For greater agility as you move up and down the court and as an aid to combatting lead-footed fatigue, use the helium device suggested for other fast-moving sports. Simply picture your shoes as being filled with helium.

Football
 • To increase passing accuracy as a quarterback, imagine an umbilical cord attached to each one of your receivers and attempt to direct the flight of the ball along this cord.
 • Kickers may find use for a couple of SyberTricks already suggested for other sports. Place kickers can enlarge the target by mentally widening the goal; punters may be more effective in trapping the opposing team close to their own goal line by mentally enlarging the "coffin corner" area inside the 10-yard line. Kickers also may be able to improve the distance of their punts and point-scoring attempts by imagining that the football is filled with helium.
 • Running backs attempting to pick a hole in the line as they charge out of the back field can use a widening tunnel effect. When they spot and run into a small hole in the defensive line they should mentally picture that aperture as a narrow entrance to a widening tunnel.
 • Defensive linemen should picture themselves as a stone wall able to thwart any assault; offensive linemen should picture themselves as battering rams, able to knock down that fortification.
 • Receivers may find themselves reaching and holding onto

more of those difficult passes if they use the helium-filled-shoes technique to get more spring and height into a leap for the ball and if they mentally enlarge the size of their hands and the size of the ball—especially the tip—for surer catches.

Racquetball
• Enlarging techniques also can work well for racquetball enthusiasts. Mentally picture a larger-than-life racquet, ball and target area.
• Mental slow-motion also can be an effective device on the racquetball court. Work at satiating all of your sensory perceptions as you mentally slow down the game.

Soccer
• In a continuous action sport such as soccer, speed and agility as well as stamina are important elements of success. Promote a lightness of foot by imagining your shoes filled with helium.
• For shooting accuracy, picture a larger goal and a smaller goal-keeper. For more effective passing and ball control, imagine the soccer ball to be larger than it actually is.

SYBERAIDS

Taste and smell sensory activation
As you have become involved in the SyberVision training program you have been introduced to a series of sensory eye-shift codes. These provide a means of access to your mental storehouse, opening specific areas of the brain for the retention, activation and creation of stored high quality performance memory. So far, you have used seven codes—for visual memory (upper left eye shift), constructed visual images (upper right), auditory memory (lateral left), constructed sounds (lateral

right), emotional memory (lower left), motion memory and body sensation recall (lower right) and sensory synthesis (central focus). Now we would like to add to your arsenal of sensory recall two additional eye-shift codes—for taste and for smell.

Although these two senses may appear to be unrelated to most sports, each is nonetheless capable of being activated to trigger that conditioned response you are looking for. Use them as follows:

Upper central eye-shift code. This eye code activates the sense of smell. Use it to associate a particularly satisfying athletic motion with your olfactory system. For example, when you bowl a strike, hit a long, straight drive off the tee or ace a serve

at tennis, code this performance into memory by inhaling a unique fragrance. This could be a distinctive cologne, or perhaps peppermint extract or eucalyptus. It should be a fragrance you don't put to everyday use and which can be reserved for your sport. Of course, it should be something that is easily transported in the pocket in a small vial or spray can. In time, a mere upper central eye-shift code will be sufficient to cue an appropriate response, with only occasional reinforcement with the actual activating fragrance.

Lower central eye-shift code. This eye code activates the sense of taste. Use it to associate the execution of a particularly pleasing sports motion with the gustatory system. Should you hit a home run, ski a flawless downhill run or make a leaping catch of the football in a big play, key into that movement with your sense of taste by flooding the palate with a distinctive flavor. Use something strong (and, of course, pleasant to the taste), such as peppermint extract, cloves or cinnamon. Again, it should be something that is convenient to carry and that is reserved exclusively for your sport. With this technique you literally get the taste of success! (Again, in time you will be able to condition the desired response simply by keying into a lower central eye-shift code.)

SyberAid to Relaxation

Part of the relaxation-oxygenation exercise detailed in Chapter Four entails using a lower right eye-shift code to mentally isolate and scan each area of the body. This occurs prior to creating tension in that body area, experiencing the release of that tension and flooding the area with the signifying color. As an aid to this scanning process, imagine a warm hand slowly exploring and sensing each area. You also can use this warm-hand technique during competition to focus on a particular area of the body where you may be experiencing tension.

Oily-joint technique

Slammin' Sam Snead always said that he liked his golf swing to feel "oily." This is an appropriate analogy, not just for golf, but for any sport where you want to gain a sense of fluid motion and dissolve stiffness. If you are experiencing stiffness during competition, you can incorporate the oily-joint technique into the oxygenation portion of your SyberVision training program.

During your Syber-Relaxation exercises (see Chapter 4), before closing out each Syber-Zone—RED, ORANGE, YELLOW—by inhaling and exhaling the colored mist, add the following:

1. **Upper right eye-shift code.** Imagine a long-spouted oil can and picture yourself applying lubrication to each joint area, working up from toes, ankles, knees, hips, etc.

2. **Lower right eye-shift code.** Use this motion memory code to feel the sensation of a very smooth and well-lubricated movement in each joint.

3. To activate during competition whenever you experience joint stiffness, simply key into the upper right eye-shift code, cue in the appropriate color and imagine that oil can lubricating

the stiff joints. You can enhance this illusion by actually flexing your legs, arms, etc., to "feel" the fluidity created by your imaginary lubrication.

You as a newsmaker

As part of your pre-competition rehearsal we suggested the mental exercise of writing an imaginary newspaper article detailing your winning performance in an upcoming match. This technique also can be applied to long term goals—such as breaking 90 at golf or bowling a 200 game—and can be a multisensory experience as follows:

1. **Upper right eye-shift code.** See yourself reading the article as it would appear when your goal is realized.

2. **Lateral right eye-shift code.** Hear friends and acquaintances who have read the article compliment you on your feat.

3. **Lower right eye-shift code.** Feel yourself actually holding the newspaper with the article about your achievement.

4. **Lower left eye-shift code.** Prelive all of the emotions—pride, joy, a sense of real accomplishment—that you would experience upon reading the article.

5. **Upper central eye-shift code.** To enhance the sense of reality, "smell" the newsprint as you read the hot-off-the-press story.

6. **Central focus.** Absorb this total experience through a synthesis of all of the senses.

As we have noted, these SyberAids and SyberTricks lend themselves both to actual competition and to training drills. In addition, they also may be incorporated into your pre-competition rehearsal (see Chapter 8).

Largo Music as a SyberAid

On the day of competition, your goal should be to feel completely relaxed and free from tension yet at the same time to maintain a threshhold of adrenalin with strong, positive self-affirmation. You have gone through your pre-game rehearsal at least 24 hours prior to the upcoming game and now you need to allow time for that sensory input to settle and take root in the brain. A relaxing session with music enhances this settling process.

Studies indicate that the slow rhythm of largo music which, at about 60 beats per minute, is in synchrony with the heartbeat, is well suited for promoting the ideal pre-competition state. Choose your tape or record, settle comfortably in an easy chair, use a lateral left eye-shift code to activate the auditory sensory mode, then close and relax your eyes and allow yourself to become totally absorbed in the music, letting your mind take flight with it.

Listen to this music for about 30 to 40 minutes two hours or so prior to competition. Some suggested selections are as follows:

J. S. Bach
  Largo Concerto in G Minor
  Aria to the Goldberg Variations
  The Greatest Hits of 1720
A. Corelli
  Corelli's Twelve Concerti Grossi, Opus 6
G. F. Handel
  Largo from Concerto No. 1
  Handel's Twelve Concerti Grossi, Opus 6
A. Vivaldi
  Largo from "Winter" From The Four Seasons

11

Recency Coding

Win or lose, perform well or play badly, post-competition dialogue typically is an enjoyable part of the casual athlete's game ritual. Golfers repair to their favorite table or stool at the "19th Hole," bowlers congregate in the lounge or coffee shop, skiers join the apres-ski crowd around a crackling log fire in the ski lodge. Conversation centers around eagle attempts narrowly missed, tough spares picked up, advanced slopes mastered for the first time. Even those who did not perform well usually have at least a few highlights to relive and savor as they sip their favorite brew.

Our objective in this chapter is to encourage post-game dialogue. The significant difference is that you will have dialogue with yourself, and it will be eminently more productive than the casual discussions you enjoy with fellow players as you rehash the day's events. Using the SyberVision coding and replay technique, you will learn how to take those superior elements of your recent performance—those same arrow-straight, long golf shots and devastating tennis volleys you enjoy reliving over the post-game beverage—and reinforce them and store them in memory.

You will recall from our discussion of competition management (see Chapter 9) that we described a simple technique using the eye-shift codes for earmarking those elements of your play that were well-executed—that looked good, felt good and produced the desired results. Now we are going to call upon your mental "tickler" system to review those superior shots or strokes for easy activation next time you play.

Remember, your objective throughout SyberVision training is to increase constantly the volume of positive muscle memory stored in your mental data bank as you strive to upscale your level of consistency. By failing to recode recent positive performance into memory you are missing out on an extremely valuable resource for future competition. Recency coding enables you to tap into that memory while it is still fresh, still sitting on the surface of your mind ready to be reinforced and recoded into memory.

Procedure For Recency Coding

1. The sooner after play or practice that you perform your recoding—while your recall remains sharp and well-defined— the more effective it will be. We recommend that you complete your recency coding session no later than 12 hours after play, preferably within six hours.

2. Seat yourself comfortably in your favorite quiet chair, just as you do for other exercises in the SyberVision program.

3. **Upper left eye-shift code.** Recall the activating colors for each of the body zones up to and including the color BLUE (do *not* enter the violet state, since you are not creating or programming, but simply storing into the right side of the brain), as follows:

RED—lower torso
ORANGE—upper torso
YELLOW—head
GREEN—left cerebral hemisphere
BLUE—right cerebral hemisphere

4. Once you reach the BLUE state, the object is to replay and reinforce mentally each positive movement from your recent performance from each of the sensory modes as follows:

a. **Upper left eye-shift code.** Replay that shot, stroke or series of well-executed motions from the visual perspective, recall what the motion looked like in as much detail as possible. Replay it five times from the internal perspective (as though you were inside that mental image of yourself) and five times from the external perspective (as though you were watching yourself perform).

b. **Lateral left eye-shift code.** Mentally replay all of the sounds associated with the motion. Recapture not only the sounds of the play itself (racket or club hitting ball, cutting edge of skis, bowling ball hitting pins, etc.), but also any background or environmental noise that is reaffirming and supportive of that motion, e.g. congratulatory comments of fellow players. Replay five times each from the internal and external perspectives.

c. **Lower left eye-shift code.** Mentally replay the motion capturing all of the positive emotions you felt while executing it—the warm glow of success, the sense of achievement. Replay five times each from the internal and external perspectives.

d. **Lower right eye-shift code.** Mentally replay the motion capturing a real sense of how it felt—the fluidity of motion and the purposeful, unhurried tempo of its execution. Use the slow-motion technique when replaying this kinesthetic mode. Replay five times each from the internal and external perspectives.

e. **Central focus eye-shift code.** Mentally replay the motion to gain a synchrony of all of the senses associated with it. Replay five times each from the internal and external perspectives.

Conclusion

1. With upper left eye-shift, slowly reverse the colors working

from blue to red, associating each color with its specific body zone. Follow each association with a lower right eye-shift.
2. With central focus eye shift, slowly open the eyes and shake out the arms and legs. At this point you will be relaxed, vitalized and clear-minded.

Use this recency coding technique to reinforce as many motions from your just-completed play as you wish to recapture in future performance. Be sure to focus upon all of the feelings, sounds and emotions associated with those motions in as much detail as possible, picking up on anything—perhaps a feeling in the arms or legs during a follow-through, an element of self-talk, a comment from a playing companion, a background sound—that you can use as a hinge for that memory.

This recency coding exercise adds the final link to the chain of events that now becomes a continuous cycle as you bring Syber-Vision techniques totally into your sport. First you enter sensory data into memory, using television sports programming or live models as a source. Next, you reinforce that data by replaying it from all of the sensory perspectives in your mental practice sessions. Then you rehearse—mentally prelive—the way you desire to perform in an upcoming competition. Then you go out and activate that pre-programmed rehearsal during competition, at the same time monitoring and mentally foot-noting moments of excellence for further reinforcement in the mind. This brings you to recency coding and then back to further input from television or from your live model as you repeat the memory-building cycle.

All the time you are constantly adding to that reservoir of stored memory, gradually filling those mental data storage banks with an ever-increasing volume of excellence as you take the best moves of the pros, of your teachers, of your opponents, partners and yourself and make them over for your own con-tinued use. And you are raising your consistency level until out

of every 100 sports motions you perform you are attaining per-
fection not in merely five, but perhaps in 10, 20, 25 or more.
You are on your way to becoming more proficient at your sport
. . . to enjoying it more and to winning more often.

12

Question and Answer Checklist

1.

Q: SyberVision seems like a natural for children. Can it be applied to children?

A: It *is* a natural for children. As you may recall, it was developed from the experience of a three-year-old child overcoming polio. Children generally have great imaginations, and they easily project themselves into the shoes—and strokes—of sports figures they admire. Most children who play sports are very receptive to the SyberVision coding techniques, and they all love to watch sports television. Using the "spoonful of sugar makes the medicine go down" philosophy, you can teach your children some of the SyberVision discipline (the medicine) using sports television as the sugar.

A child who has learned some elements of SyberVision will have acquired a mental framework and discipline which will help him in most undertakings, including his studies. The SyberMan/SyberWoman and the "Bad Bug" (known to us adults as SyberDemon) can be used creatively in childrearing, not to intimidate the child but to help him build confidence in himself.

2.

Q: When I use my eye shift codes, I seem to get tension headaches. How do I avoid this?

A: If you hold your eyes in any of the coding positions for too long, you will probably get a slight tension headache. Your eye movements should be slow, gentle glides. When you reach the appropriate position, hold that position for a few seconds, then release and let the eyes return to normal. In the normal position, you can process or recall the information you need. The important thing is that you signal the brain with the appropriate eye code prior to sensory input and recall.

3.

Q: Why the specific choice of colors for relaxation? Don't some colors, like red, cause tension?

A: Some research indicates that we unconsciously respond to colors in predictable ways. According to this research, the fire colors, like red and orange, may cause tension. Our position is that, if we are in control, if we ascribe a certain meaning to a color through conditioning, that color will activate the response we want. The philosophy of the SyberVision program is that of self-control. The winning athlete controls his responses to environment. The losing athlete is controlled by environmental stimuli.

4.

Q: How long should I wear my eye patch?

A: We recommend that, if you are cross dominant (right-eyed, left-handed; left-eyed, right-handed), you wear your Syber-Vision patch over your dominant eye at least two hours per day for 30 days and one hour per day thereafter. You should also use your patch when you are doing your eye/hand coordination exercises, alternating eyes as prescribed in the book.

5.

Q: How long should I continue my eye/hand coordination exercises?

A: You should continue your exercises until they have lost their challenge for you. If you find the exercises are too easy, then be creative and invent your own. We are in the process of completing an advanced eye/hand coordination exercise booklet with an exercise schedule for eye/hand coordination conditioning.

6.

Q: I have a hard time seeing the colors. What should I do?

A: It is not necessary to "see" the colors inside your head. Very few people can actually see the colors. All you must do is "sense" or remember what the colors look like. By sensing or remembering the colors, instead of forcing them to mind, you will find your color cues more accessible to you.

7.

Q: When I do my Syber-Relaxation Exercises at night, I usually fall asleep. How can I avoid this?

A: This result is great if you're an insomniac. If you're not, then you're probably doing your Syber Sessions in bed, prior to going to sleep. Doing this, you are conditioning your eye shift codes and colors to put you to sleep. In the evening, instead of doing your exercises in bed, do them in a chair before you get tired. By doing this you will find that sleep will not interfere with your session. Then, after your session, you will sleep like a baby.

8.

Q: When I watch my favorite sports on television, the action is so fast that I can't recall it for my coding exercises. Is T.V. coding really possible?

A: Yes, it is possible. Your brain can and will process all of the sensory information fed back to it by the television, activating your quality performance memories. However, without the SyberVision memory codes, your access to those activated performance memories will be random and your sports performance inconsistent.

If you don't have a video tape recorder, you should try to focus your attention on a specific motion, untangling that motion from all of the action on the screen, and then coding it into your brain. If you have a video tape recorder, you can record the sports action from your television and then play it back over and over at regular speed and in slow motion (if your video tape recorder is so equipped), coding the motion into your brain as you watch.

9.

Q: It's difficult for me to remember the exact steps in the oxygenation and brain coding process. Is there an easier way than having to hold the book in my hand as I go through the process?

A: If you have a hard time remembering each step in the process, you could record each step on an audio cassette tape and play back each step. Put the recorder on pause, and perform the instruction. Once you can perform the steps from memory, do not rely on the tape—remember, you should be in control at all times.

10.

Q: How long will it take to start getting results from Syber-Vision?

A: If you follow the program exactly as outlined, if you make it into a strict discipline, you will begin to see dramatic performance results within 30 days. If you apply the program casually, taking the easy way out, your results will be noticeable, but also elusive—not consistent all the time—hot and cold. The SyberVision discipline gives you the control and consistency you need to excel at your sport. It is up to you to use that discipline effectively.

11.

Q: Each sport is so unique in nature. How can SyberVision be applied to every sport?

A: SyberVision can be applied to any endeavor in which consistency in executing a skill or a set of skills is of prime importance.

Each sport does have its unique nature. Some sports are fast-moving, like basketball and soccer, while others are solitary, such as golf or bowling, with few variables other than the player and his immediate environment. Most sports are a combination of the two. But all sports have one characteristic in common. They are all based on fundamental skills that have to be mastered before the sport can be enjoyed or before the athlete can be productive. It is this fundamental consistency to which SyberVision addresses itself.

12.

Q: Does SyberVision have a scientific basis?

A: The strength of SyberVision is that it is both practical and scientifically sound. Every step in the process can be explained by a proven scientific principle. SyberVision is the only sports training discipline that defines relaxation and concentration operationally, in psychological and physiological terms.

The SyberVision brain coding technique is the practical application of a theory developed by one of the most renowned and respected brain researchers in the world: Dr. Karl Pribram, of Stanford University.

Dr. Pribram's work on brain processes has had a profound impact on the brain and psychological sciences and is likely to revolutionize man's perception of himself in the course of the 1980's.

13.

Q: Is SyberVision hypnosis?

A: Definitely not.

14.

Q: Can SyberVision be applied to areas outside of sports?

A: Yes. We are now conducting extensive research applying the principles of SyberVision to the health field, management, industrial training, education, the military, and personal development. We will be presenting books, video and audio cassette programs in these areas very shortly.

15.

Q: Couldn't SyberVision be dangerous if it fell into the wrong hands?

A: SyberVision is a powerful tool for change and improvement. Like any new technology or invention, it can be used for good or evil purposes. Our hope is that it will be utilized for the benefit of mankind. We are committed to that effort.

16.

Q: When I have questions about SyberVision or would like to share my SyberVision experience, to whom can I direct my communications?

A: We will attempt to answer all questions regarding the application of SyberVision, if they are mailed with a self-addressed, stamped envelope to P.D.A., 2450 Washington Avenue, Suite 220, San Leandro, CA 94577.

If you have had a successful experience you would like to share, we would like to hear about that too. We will select such questions and experience as reference material for our Syber-Vision Newsletter, *The Sports Psychologist*, and other future publications. For every experience we use in any of our publications, we will send along a free SyberVision Muscle Memory Power T-Shirt to the person submitting the information.

13

SyberVision 30-Day Mastery Schedule

As we have stressed repeatedly throughout this book, Syber-Vision training is not something to be rushed. It is not a magic elixir that will transform a weekend athlete into a sports super-star. Nor will it overnight produce dramatic improvements in your game.

SyberVision is a discipline based on sound scientific prin-ciples. It is a whole new mental approach to sports training that must be given time to take root and grow within you. Given time and dedicated application—because you must make a commitment to work at mastering the SyberVision exercises and techniques—it does have the remarkable potential to increase your consistency at a given sport and thus improve your overall performance and your ability to win.

Each chapter of this book presents a detailed explanation of a separate segment of the total SyberVision approach to sports training—relaxation, concentration, pre-competition rehearsal, competition management, etc. As you progress through the book, you will find that each segment of the program dovetails into the others as you build a total system of muscle memory power. The object of this SyberVision Mastery Schedule is to demonstrate how these segments interlock, day-by-day, over a 30-day period from Day 1 through Day 30.

If you are serious about wanting to improve your performance at your favorite sports we urge you to follow this program as closely as possible. The final value you receive from the SyberVision system of muscle memory programming will depend on how many of its applications, insights and guidelines you can, or choose to, adopt as habit-knit skills in your endeavor to maximize your sports potential.

STEPS TO MUSCLE MEMORY POWER

Before outlining your 30-day SyberVision Mastery Schedule, we will briefly review each of the segments that make up the total muscle-memory training program. These building blocks of SyberVision are:

1. EYE-HAND COORDINATION (CHAPTER 2)

OBJECTIVE
You will be able to sharpen your eye-hand coordination for increased sport consistency.

Background
Eye-hand coordination is the ability of the eye and body to work together in a coordinated effort. The eye aligns the body and receives incoming information that must be acted upon or reacted to by the body.

Eye-hand coordination is inherent or natural if the dominant eye and the dominant side of the body coincide. If your right eye is dominant and you are right-handed, or your left eye is dominant and you are left-handed, then your are naturally aligned. You have the potential for a greater degree of consistency in your sport performance. If you are cross dominant (right eye—left handed, left eye—right handed), then you will experience extreme fluctuations in consistency.

You can determine your dominant eye by taking a simple alignment test (page 23). If you are cross dominant, you can train your subordinate eye to begin to process vital alignment information. Whether you are or are not naturally aligned, you can increase your eye-hand coordination by following prescribed exercises outlined in Chapter 2.

2. EYE CODING TECHNIQUES (CHAPTER 3)

OBJECTIVE
You will be able to activate each of the seven eye shift positions to gain access into the brain for input and output of sensory-rich muscle memory.

Background

Every sports-related movement you have ever made is rich in sensory information—sight, sound, touch and emotion. Your brain has the ability to record, store and play back all of the experiences and information you encounter through your senses. While your brain can randomly record muscle memory information gained through the senses, you have lacked a controlled and orderly way to have access to that stored muscle (sensory) memory for consistency in sports performance. Whenever you haphazardly draw up stored sensory memory, your eyes have a revealing pattern of movement that shows from what area of the brain you are retrieving these stored data and what senses you are activating.

Using these patterns of eye movements, you can create door knobs or entry codes to each of the sensory areas of the brain. These codes or eye movements will provide easy access to your muscle memory storehouse of pure, fundamentally sound movement. The eye shift patterns will allow you to open up areas of your brain for recording, storing and recalling high-quality muscle memory.

3. SYBER-RELAXATION (CHAPTER 4)

OBJECTIVE
Activating certain eye-shift codes and colors that represent different muscle groups, you will be able to signal your brain to send oxygen-rich blood to any muscle group that you desire to relax.

Background
Relaxation is the foundation of consistent sports performance. Without it you cannot expect your muscles to respond fluidly and automatically to the intent of your mind. Oxygen is the life force of muscle tissue. When you are tense, as a result of a fear of failure or any other type of doubt, this tension constricts blood vessels leading to muscle tissue, cutting off, restricting vital oxygen to muscle tissue. This lack of oxygen curtails supple, refined movement and endurance.

The SyberVision system of muscle relaxation is a discipline that allows you to become sensitive to muscle binding tension and to automatically oxygenate your muscle tissue by simply using your eye-shift codes and recalling a series of color cues. To make the oxygenation process automatic (activating blood flow to a muscle group with a simple eye movement), will take approximately two weeks, two times per day, of following the program outlined in Chapter 4. (Refer also to SyberVision Mastery Schedule that follows this program review.) To maximize the effectiveness of the SyberVision Muscle Memory Programming process it is necessary to master the oxygenation Syber-Relaxation Technique.

4. SYBER-CONCENTRATION (CHAPTER 5)

OBJECTIVE
You will be able to groove a single-minded channel to and from the brain through which the impulses representing pure movement can travel through your nervous system to activate relaxed and primed muscle tissue for precise and coordinated movement.

Background

Concentration is your ability to tap into your sensory-rich muscle memory and to open up a single sensory tract through which the memory can flow from your brain's storage banks to your muscles.

Your brain already carries stored data on all of the correct body actions and all of the feelings, emotions, sights and sounds that accompany these perfectly executed movements. The problem is, you simply can't call up the precise information when you need it. Using the Syber-Concentration technique, you will be able to effectively enter and store into specific areas of your brain the memory of perfect form. And you'll learn how to stimulate and activate it during actual play for increased consistency.

Knowing precisely in what areas of your brain sensory muscle memory is stored will help you to improve your muscle memory storage and recall.

Functionally, your brain is developed into two sections, the left cerebral hemisphere and the right cerebral hemisphere. The hemispheres resemble a walnut shell. Deep within the hemispheres, holding the two sides together, is the corpus callosum, a structure of nervous tissue and fiber that acts as a bridge for the transfer of electrical impulses and information-sharing between the left and right cerebral hemispheres. The left cerebral hemisphere is the thinking side of your brain. Its function is rational and logical thinking, verbal, analytical and strategic processing. The left side of your brain, is, in essence, the thinking you. It handles your planning, organizing and directing abilities.

Your right cerebral hemisphere handles non-verbal functions and the processing of sensory information relating to sight, sound, touch, smell, taste and emotion—sensory muscle memory. The right side of your brain is the source of instinctive, automatic, conditioned reflexes.

The corpus callosum allows for the interaction of your left and right cerebral hemispheres. The left hemisphere formulates the goal, sets the strategy, and directs the right brain to act automatically. After the right brain acts, the left brain analyzes and assesses the movement.

5. YOUR TELEVISION AS A LABORATORY OF LEARNING (CHAPTER 6)

OBJECTIVE
You will be able to process and use televised playback of your favorite sport to activate and reinforce your muscle memory.

Background
Televised playback of your favorite sport, if processed properly (utilizing the SyberVision formula for muscle memory programming), can stimulate that five percent or so of fundamentally sound muscle memory you have stored in your brain.

This televised feedback is a catalyst that affects all of the senses—sight, sound, touch, feeling and emotion. It will enable you to plug the computer in your mind into the action on your television screen.

You will take the sensory input from your television screen and put it into your memory at a frequency where it will resonate with previously stored memory and where it can be activated as needed when you go out to play the sport yourself. By following the SyberVision formula for television coding, you can use televised sports programming to electronically build your proficiency level from the hypothetical five percent to whatever level it is within your capability to accomplish.

6. USING SYBERVISION TO GET THE MOST OUT OF INSTRUCTION (CHAPTER 7)

OBJECTIVE
You will be able to apply the SyberVision Muscle Memory Programming formula to get the most out of sport instruction.

Background

It is not the intent of SyberVision to equip you with the fundamentals of your sport. There are many excellent books and professional instruction that detail the fundamental complexities of your sport. It is easy to *tell* someone how he or she should execute complex movements and to provide the rationale behind such explanations. But putting that detailed knowledge into action is the difficult part. Many instructors take beginning and intermediate athletes and infuse them with sensory-rich negative feedback of their performance.

Negative feedback is helpful if it is applied intelligently in small doses and for fine tuning and refinement. But it does have a major drawback. In an attempt to be helpful, this approach lengthens the training time required to master fundamentals and to create good muscle memory habits. It causes frustration and tension. If you are at the 5% proficiency level, your brain already knows how to perform the fundamentally sound motion. When you seek professional instruction, look for the pro who uses himself or herself as a visual and sensory model. It pays to search for the pro who is prepared to review your game and to recognize, emphasize and reinforce your 5% proficiency level. With this type of instruction you can apply the SyberVision Muscle Memory Programming formula to create a high level of consistency—a reservoir of rich, habitual muscle memory.

7. PRE-COMPETITION REHEARSAL (CHAPTER 8)

OBJECTIVE
You will be able to pre-program your muscle memory for increasing consistency in play and competition.

Background
Prior to your weekly sport play or competition, you will use the dynamics of SyberVision to stage in rich mental detail a pre-competition sensory rehearsal. Just as in show business, before you take your act on the road you will have a full dress rehearsal staged in your mind. You will program into your sensory computer specific desired future performance. And, when you go out to play, you can activate that stored memory.

You will stage your pre-competition rehearsal 18 to 24 hours prior to your event. This will allow for your programmed sensory performance to ferment, to take root in your brain, nervous system and muscles.

In the left side of your brain, you will program your game strategy and performance goals. In the right side of the brain, you will activate and replay all of the rich sensory memory you have inputted into your brain following the SyberVision program—from television, from instruction and from using superior players as models. Using the bridge between the left brain and the right brain (the corpus callosum), you will combine both sides of the brain to work in harmony. You will project your performance into your future event and pre-live it in succinct strategy and sensory detail.

8. COMPETITION MANAGEMENT (CHAPTER 9)

OBJECTIVE
You will be able to activate all of your previously stored rich sensory memory in competition—putting your muscle memory on "auto pilot".

Background
You have learned how to relax and how to concentrate. Modeling from performances of professional and top amateurs you watch on television and from sport instructors, you have activated and enlarged your storehouse of positive muscle memory. You know how the fundamental motions that lead to consistent high performance look, sound, feel. And, you have rehearsed, in exquisite sensory detail, the competition in which you will be engaging.

By simply activating an eye-shift code and a color, you will be able to trigger all of that stored and programmed muscle memory. Merely by pressing the start button, your mental computer will take and direct all of your movement. You will be on auto-pilot. Your nervous system has already performed the feat; you must merely recreate it naturally. When you encounter a situation in competition that creates tension and doubt, you can control the performance-detracting tension by associating the tension with a negative symbol—a cartoon caricature we call SyberDemon, and by associating the opposite of tension—confidence—with a positive symbol we call SyberMan or Syber-Woman.

9. RECENCY CODING (CHAPTER 11)

OBJECTIVE
After a match or game, to take the best elements of your performance and reinforce them in memory.

Background
During play you will use eye-shift codes for earmarking those elements of your play that were well-executed—that looked good, felt good and produced the desired results. Recency coding is a technique for mentally reviewing those superior shots or strokes for activation next time you play. If you did it correctly one, you can do it again! This recoding should be performed as soon after play as possible—while your recall remains sharp and well-defined. Ideally, your recency coding session should occur within six hours of play; certainly no later than 12 hours following performance. Recency coding is the final link in the chain of events that now becomes a continuous cycle as you embody SyberVision techniques totally into your sport.

BEFORE YOU BEGIN
YOUR 30-DAY MASTERY SCHEDULE

1. Check your eye dominance:

a. Take the simple Test For Dominance (page 23), to determine whether you are right-side dominant or left-side dominant or whether you are cross-dominant.

b. After taking the eye dominance test, check your results in the space provided below:

RIGHT-EYED—RIGHT-HANDED_____

LEFT-EYED—RIGHT-HANDED_____

LEFT-EYED—LEFT-HANDED_____

RIGHT-EYED—LEFT-HANDED_____

c. If you are cross-dominant (left-eyed—right-handed, right-eyed—left-handed), you may lack the natural ability to align with a target. In this case, you'll need to train your "lazy eye." To get the lazy eye to take up more of the workload, begin wearing a patch over the dominant eye during sports practice and even around the home for an hour or two each day. This places the burden of alignment onto the other eye and allows you to build a more natural eye-body coordination.

2. Study and Master the SyberVision Eye-Coding Positions (refer to chart, page 34)

a. Study the eye-shift patterns on the chart and become thoroughly familiar with each position and its corresponding function in recalling and constructing certain sensory memories. Note that there are seven basic positions to learn: 1. UPPER LEFT—external and internal visual memory; 2. UPPER RIGHT—construction of visual images and symbols; 3. LATERAL LEFT—auditory memory; 4. LATERAL RIGHT—construction of sounds and words; 5. LOWER LEFT—emotional memory and feeling; 6. LOWER RIGHT—motion memory and body sensation recall; 7. CENTRAL FOCUS—sensory synthesis. Note: the chart provided and the positions just described apply to a *right-handed* person. If you are *left-handed,* the most common tendency is for the field of *visual* processing to be the reverse of those for the right-hand dominant person (reverse the two upper eye shifts *only*) while everything else remains the same.

b. Demonstrate to yourself how eye-shift patterns really are "doorknobs to the mind" by completing the SyberVision Sensory Eye Shift Code Charting Questionnaire (page 35). You'll find that it's fun to do (especially with a friend—try it as a party trick) as well as extremely revealing.

3. **Preparing Your Own SyberVision Training Place:**

a. Choose the area in the home that will serve as your "quiet place" for SyberVision training. Ideal would be a den or study with a comfortable reclining chair and a television set for your television encoding sessions. However, any quiet spot will serve—perhaps a corner of a bedroom or family room that is away from the traffic flow in the home and where you will be free from noise, interruptions and other distractions.

b. Set up your color recall charts for the six SyberVision colors—RED, ORANGE, YELLOW, GREEN, BLUE and VIOLET. You may wish to temporarily mount color panels (about one-foot square) on a wall facing your SyberVision training area. Or, as a smaller, portable aid you might follow our suggestion of clipping color chips from a paint dealer's sample sheet and mounting each color on a separate 4 x 5 index card. A third, although less desirable, alternative is to simply use ingrained objects to help you cue into each color, e.g. an apple, an orange, a lemon, for the colors red, orange and yellow.

Now you are ready to begin DAY ONE of your SyberVision training program.

DAY ONE

1. Spend 10 minutes studying the eye-shift patterns on the coding chart and practicing the various eye shifts. For practice, use the SyberVision Sensory Eye Shift Code Charting Questionnaire (page 35), simply answering the questions to yourself and, as you do, apply the corresponding eye movements. As you search sensory memory to respond to each question, you should become aware of your eye movement.

2. Spend 15-30 minutes working at the Hand-Eye Coordination Exercises (see page 25). Choose from SyberJacks, SyberStraws, SyberChopsticks, SyberPitchback, SyberDarts, Putting and SyberAim. (Optional)

3. If you are cross-dominant, spend an hour or two wearing a patch over your dominant eye to encourage the lazy eye to become accustomed to doing its share of the work. (Optional)

4. Spend a few minutes practicing the Color Recall Exercise for the first three SyberVision colors—red, orange and yellow (see page 47).

5. Complete BASIC SYBER-RELAXATION EXERCISE— do this *twice daily*.

CHECKLIST   *time spent*
☐ STUDY EYE-SHIFT CHART   _____
☐ PRACTICE WITH EYE-SHIFT
   QUESTIONNAIRE   _____
☐ HAND-EYE COORDINATION EXERCISES
(your choice of one or more of the following):
   SYBERJACKS   _____
   SYBERSTRAWS   _____
   SYBERCHOPSTICKS   _____
   SYBERPITCHBACK   _____
   SYBERDARTS   _____
   PUTTING   _____
   SYBERAIM   _____
☐ COLOR RECALL EXERCISE   _____
☐ BASIC SYBERRELAXATION EXERCISE   _____

DAY TWO

1. Spend 10 minutes studying and practicing eye-shift patterns. TIP: When practicing eye shifts using the questionnaire, strive to recall and create your mental pictures in as much sensory detail as possible.

2. Spend 15-30 minutes working at the Hand-Eye Coordination Exercises. (Optional)

3. If you are cross-dominant, work with your eye patch for an hour or two. (Optional)

4. Spend a few minutes practicing the Color Recall Exercise.

5. Complete BASIC SYBER-RELAXATION EXERCISE—do this twice daily. TIP: If you have any kind of injury—back, shoulder, leg, etc.—be sure not to tense that region of the body beyond the threshhold of pain. Remember, pain is the body's warning to cease and desist.

CHECKLIST	*time spent*
☐ STUDY EYE-SHIFT CHART	_____
☐ PRACTICE WITH EYE-SHIFT QUESTIONNAIRE	_____
☐ HAND-EYE COORDINATION EXERCISES	
(your choice of one or more of the following):	
SYBERJACKS	_____
SYBERSTRAWS	_____
SYBERCHOPSTICKS	_____
SYBERPITCHBACK	_____
SYBERDARTS	_____
PUTTING	_____
SYBERAIM	_____
☐ COLOR RECALL EXERCISE	_____
☐ BASIC SYBERRELAXATION EXERCISE	_____

DAY THREE

1. Spend 10 minutes studying and practicing eye-shift patterns.

2. Spend 15-30 minutes working at the Hand-Eye Coordination Exercises. (Optional) TIP: For variety, you may wish to tackle the seven suggested exercises one-a-day over a period of a week.

3. If you are cross-dominant, work with your eye patch for an hour or two. (Optional)

4. Spend a few minutes practicing the Color Recall Exercise. TIP: The more you practice this exercise, the easier it will become to quickly recall these colors. The concept of recalling colors is the first step toward establishing the ability to relax as a conditioned reflex. It also is a honing tool that will help you put a cutting edge on your powers of concentration.

5. Complete BASIC SYBER-RELAXATION EXERCISE—do this twice daily.

CHECKLIST   *time spent*

☐ STUDY EYE-SHIFT CHART   _____
☐ PRACTICE WITH EYE-SHIFT
   QUESTIONNAIRE   _____
☐ HAND-EYE COORDINATION EXERCISES
(your choice of one or more of the following):
     SYBERJACKS   _____
     SYBERSTRAWS   _____
     SYBERCHOPSTICKS   _____
     SYBERPITCHBACK   _____
     SYBERDARTS   _____
     PUTTING   _____
     SYBERAIM   _____
☐ COLOR RECALL EXERCISE   _____
☐ BASIC SYBERRELAXATION EXERCISE _____

DAY FOUR

1. Spend 10 minutes studying and practicing eye-shift patterns. TIP: Be careful not to exaggerate eye shifts. While these should be distinct movements in the directions indicated, they also should be fleeting, almost imperceptible movements.

2. Spend 15-30 minutes working at the Hand-Eye Coordination Exercises. (Optional)

3. If you are cross-dominant, work with your eye patch for an hour or two. (Optional)

4. Spend a few minutes practicing the Color Recall Exercise. TIP: As you concentrate on mentally recalling each color, do not expect that color to blaze into the mind. Very few persons are such keen visualizers. Simply try to recall in your mind a sense of what each color looks like.

5. Complete BASIC SYBER-RELAXATION EXERCISE—do this twice daily.

CHECKLIST   *time spent*

☐ STUDY EYE-SHIFT CHART   _____
☐ PRACTICE WITH EYE-SHIFT
     QUESTIONNAIRE   _____
☐ HAND-EYE COORDINATION EXERCISES
(your choice of one or more of the following):
     SYBERJACKS   _____
     SYBERSTRAWS   _____

SYBERCHOPSTICKS   ———
SYBERPITCHBACK   ———
SYBERDARTS   ———
PUTTING   ———
SYBERAIM   ———
□ COLOR RECALL EXERCISE   ———
□ BASIC SYBERRELAXATION EXERCISE   ———

DAY FIVE

1. Spend 10 minutes studying and practicing eye-shift patterns.

2. Spend 15-30 minutes working at the Hand-Eye Coordination Exercises. (Optional)

3. If you are cross-dominant, work with your eye patch for an hour or two. (Optional)

4. Spend a few minutes practicing the Color Recall Exercise.

5. Complete BASIC SYBER-RELAXATION EXERCISE—do this twice daily. TIP: Be sure to dress comfortably in loose-fitting clothing and to remove any object that you can sense as being weighty or binding—shoes, glasses, watch, rings, belt, etc. You need to feel totally unrestricted.

CHECKLIST

time spent

□ STUDY EYE-SHIFT CHART   ———
□ PRACTICE WITH EYE-SHIFT
   QUESTIONNAIRE   ———

☐ HAND-EYE COORDINATION EXERCISES
(your choice of one or more of the following):
    SYBERJACKS   _____
    SYBERSTRAWS   _____
    SYBERCHOPSTICKS   _____
    SYBERDARTS   _____
    SYBERPITCHBACK   _____
    SYBERDARTS   _____
    PUTTING   _____
    SYBERAIM   _____
☐ COLOR RECALL EXERCISE   _____
☐ BASIC SYBERRELAXATION EXERCISE   _____

DAY SIX

1. Spend 10 minutes studying and practicing eye-shift patterns.

2. Spend 15-30 minutes working at the Hand-Eye Coordination Exercises. (Optional)

3. If you are cross-dominant, work with your eye patch for an hour or two. (Optional)

4. Spend a few minutes practicing the Color Recall Exercise. NOTE: By now, you should be sufficiently adept at recalling the three conditioning colors red, orange and yellow. After today, this exercise may be omitted from your daily program.

5. Complete BASIC SYBER-RELAXATION EXERCISE—do this twice daily.

CHECKLIST   *time spent*

☐ STUDY EYE-SHIFT CHART   ————
☐ PRACTICE WITH EYE-SHIFT
   QUESTIONNAIRE   ————
☐ HAND-EYE COORDINATION EXERCISES
(your choice of one or more of the following):
   SYBERJACKS   ————
   SYBERSTRAWS   ————
   SYBERPITCHBACK   ————
   SYBERDARTS   ————
   PUTTING   ————
   SYBERAIM   ————
☐ COLOR RECALL EXERCISE   ————
☐ BASIC SYBERRELAXATION EXERCISE   ————

———————————————————————————————————————

DAY SEVEN

1. Spend 10 minutes studying and practicing eye-shift patterns.
NOTE: By now, you should be totally familiar with these eye-
shift codes. After today, this exercise may be omitted from your
daily schedule. However, we do recommend that you do this
exercise once a week—at least during the first few weeks of
SyberVision training—as a refresher.

2. Spend 15-30 minutes working at the Hand-Eye Coordination
Exercises. (Optional)

3. If you are cross-dominant, work with your eye patch for an
hour or two. (Optional)

4. Complete BASIC SYBER-RELAXATION EXERCISE—do
this twice daily.

CHECKLIST   *time spent*

☐ STUDY EYE-SHIFT CHART   _____
☐ PRACTICE WITH EYE-SHIFT
   QUESTIONNAIRE   _____
☐ HAND-EYE COORDINATION EXERCISES
(your choice of one or more of the following):
   SYBERJACKS   _____
   SYBERSTRAWS   _____
   SYBERCHOPSTICKS   _____
   SYBERPITCHBACK   _____
   SYBERDARTS   _____
   PUTTING   _____
   SYBERAIM   _____
☐ BASIC SYBERRELAXATION EXERCISE   _____

DAY EIGHT

1. Spend 15-30 minutes working at the Hand-Eye Coordination Exercises. (Optional)

2. If you are cross-dominant, work with your eye patch for an hour or two. (Optional)

3. Complete BASIC SYBER-RELAXATION EXERCISE—do this twice daily. TIP: If, during the tensing portion of the exercise, you experience a cramp—the legs usually are particularly susceptible—don't panic. Instead, try this visual technique: Imagine the constricted muscle as a hard, cold ball of butter. Then, imagine a warm flow of blood flooding into the muscle, melting the butter, dissolving the cramp.

CHECKLIST   *time spent*

☐ HAND-EYE COORDINATION EXERCISES
(your choice of one or more of the following):

    SYBERJACKS   ―――――
    SYBERSTRAWS   ―――――
    SYBERCHOPSTICKS   ―――――
    SYBERPITCHBACK   ―――――
    SYBERDARTS   ―――――
    PUTTING   ―――――
    SYBERAIM   ―――――
☐ BASIC SYBERRELAXATION EXERCISE   ―――――

DAY NINE

1. Spend 15-30 minutes working at the Hand-Eye Coordination Exercises. (Optional)

2. If you are cross-dominant, work with your eye patch for an hour or two. (Optional)

3. Complete BASIC SYBER-RELAXATION EXERCISE—do this twice daily. TIP: Some Sybervision students prefer to do their evening relaxation exercise while lying in bed. The danger in this is that you are conditioning your eye-shift codes and colors to put you to sleep. It is better to do your exercises in a chair, before you get tired. By doing this you will find that sleep will not interfere with your session. Then, after your session, you will sleep like a baby.

CHECKLIST   *time spent*

☐ **HAND-EYE COORDINATION EXERCISES**
(your choice of one or more of the following):
      SYBERJACKS   _____
      SYBERSTRAWS   _____
      SYBERCHOPSTICKS   _____
      SYBERPITCHBACK   _____
      SYBERDARTS   _____
      PUTTING   _____
      SYBERAIM   _____
☐ **BASIC SYBERRELAXATION EXERCISE**

DAY TEN

1. Spend 15-30 minutes working at the Hand-Eye Coordination
Exercises. (Optional)

2. If you are cross-dominant, work with your eye patch for an
hour or two. (Optional)

3. Complete BASIC SYBER-RELAXATION EXERCISE—do
this twice daily. NOTE: After today, you should be ready to
switch from this BASIC relaxation exercise to the abbreviated
INTERMEDIATE exercise and add to your daily regimen the
SYBER-CONCENTRATION exercise. (However, you w
continue to do the full BASIC program once a week.)

CHECKLIST   ti

☐ **HAND-EYE COORDINATION EXERCISES**
(your choice of one or more of the following):

SYBERJACKS   _____
SYBERSTRAWS   _____
SYBERCHOPSTICKS   _____
SYBERPITCHBACK   _____
SYBERDARTS   _____
PUTTING   _____
SYBERAIM   _____
☐ BASIC SYBERRELAXATION EXERCISE   _____

DAY ELEVEN

1. Spend 15-30 minutes working at the Hand-Eye Coordination Exercises. (Optional)

2. If you are cross-dominant, work with your eye patch for an hour or two. (Optional)

3. Complete INTERMEDIATE SYBER-RELAXATION EXERCISE—do this twice daily. This simply is an abbreviated version of the basic relaxation exercise that you have completed during the first 10 days of this Mastery Schedule with certain portions either eliminated or condensed.

4. *Immediately following* the Intermediate Syber-Relaxation Exercise complete the BASIC SYBER-CONCENTRATION XERCISE; simply tag it onto the end.

ᐧLIST   *time spent*

EYE COORDINATION EXERCISES
of one or more of the following):
CKS   _____

SYBERSTRAWS   _____
SYBERCHOPSTICKS   _____
SYBERPITCHBACK   _____
SYBERDARTS   _____
PUTTING   _____
SYBERAIM   _____
☐ INTERMEDIATE SYBERRELAXATION
EXERCISE   _____
☐ BASIC SYBERCONCENTRATION
EXERCISE   _____

DAY TWELVE

1. Spend 15-30 minutes working at the Hand-Eye Coordination Exercises. (Optional)

2. If you are cross-dominant, work with your eye patch for an hour or two. (Optional)

3. Complete INTERMEDIATE SYBER-RELAXATION EXERCISE—do this twice daily followed by SYBER-CONCENTRATION (below).

4. Immediately following the Intermediate Syber-Relaxation Exercise complete the BASIC SYBER-CONCENTRATION EXERCISE; simply tag it onto the end.

5. Spend a few minutes practicing the Color Recall Exercise. NOTE: This now comprises of the *six* SyberVision color cues. To the initial colors red, orange and yellow, you now have added green, blue and violet.

CHECKLIST   *time spent*

☐ HAND-EYE COORDINATION EXERCISES   _____
☐ INTERMEDIATE SYBERRELAXATION
   EXERCISE   _____
☐ BASIC SYBER-CONCENTRATION
   EXERCISE   _____
☐ COLOR RECALL EXERCISE   _____

DAY THIRTEEN

1. Spend 15-30 minutes working at the Hand-Eye Coordination Exercises. (Optional)

2. If you are cross-dominant, work with your eye patch for an hour or two. (Optional)

3. Complete INTERMEDIATE SYBER-RELAXATION EXERCISE—do this twice daily followed by SYBER-CONCENTRATION (below).

4. Immediately following the Intermediate Syber-Relaxation Exercise complete the BASIC SYBER-CONCENTRATION EXERCISE; simply tag it onto the end.

5. Spend a few minutes practicing the Color Recall Exercise (six colors).

6. Try your first television coding session (see chapter six). Ideally, this should occur on a weekend when there are plenty of televised sports programs to choose from. Remember, don't rush out immediately after your television input session to see if

it works! Spend a week mentally practicing these "TV tapes" before you go out to play.

CHECKLIST   *time spent*

☐ HAND-EYE COORDINATION EXERCISES   _____
☐ INTERMEDIATE SYBERRELAXATION
    EXERCISE   _____
☐ BASIC SYBER-CONCENTRATION
    EXERCISE   _____
☐ COLOR RECALL EXERCISE   _____
☐ TV CODING SESSION   _____

_____

DAY FOURTEEN

1. Spend 15-30 minutes working at the Hand-Eye Coordination Exercises. (Optional)

2. If you are cross-dominant, work with your eye patch for an hour or two. (Optional)

3. As a refresher, spend 10 minutes studying and practicing eye-shift patterns.

4. Complete INTERMEDIATE SYBER-RELAXATION EXERCISE—do this twice daily followed by SYBER-CONCENTRATION (below).

5. Immediately following the Intermediate Syber-Relaxation Exercise complete the BASIC SYBER-CONCENTRATION EXERCISE: simply tag it onto the end.

6. Spend a few minutes practicing the Color Recall Exercise (six colors).

7. Practice the "mental tapes" you made during your TV coding session.

CHECKLIST   *time spent*

☐ HAND-EYE COORDINATION EXERCISES   _____
☐ STUDY EYE-SHIFT CHART
☐ INTERMEDIATE SYBERRELAXATION
   EXERCISE   _____
☐ BASIC SYBER-CONCENTRATION
   EXERCISE   _____
☐ COLOR RECALL EXERCISE   _____
☐ PRACTICE TV MENTAL TAPES   _____

DAY FIFTEEN

1. Spend 15-30 minutes working at the Hand-Eye Coordination Exercises (Optional)

2. If you are cross-dominant, work with the eye patch for an hour or two. (Optional)

3. Complete INTERMEDIATE SYBER-RELAXATION EXERCISE—do this twice daily followed by SYBER-CONCENTRATION (below).

4. Immediately following the Intermediate Syber-Relaxation Exercise complete the BASIC SYBER-CONCENTRATION EXERCISE; simply tag it onto the end.

5. Spend a few minutes practicing the Color Recall Exercise (six colors).

6. Practice the "mental tapes" you made during your TV coding session.

CHECKLIST   *time spent*
☐ HAND-EYE COORDINATION EXERCISES   _____
☐ INTERMEDIATE SYBERRELAXATION
   EXERCISE   _____
☐ BASIC SYBER-CONCENTRATION
   EXERCISE   _____
☐ COLOR RECALL EXERCISE
☐ PRACTICE TV MENTAL TAPES   _____

DAY SIXTEEN

1. Spend 15-30 minutes working at the Hand-Eye Coordination Exercises. (Optional)

2. If you are cross-dominant, work with your eye patch for an hour or two. (Optional)

3. Complete INTERMEDIATE SYBER-RELAXATION EXERCISE—do this twice daily followed by SYBER-CONCENTRATION (below)

4. Immediately following the Intermediate Syber-Relaxation Exercise complete the BASIC SYBER-CONCENTRATION EXERCISE; simply tag it onto the end.

5. Spend a few minutes practicing the Color Recall Exercise (six colors).

6. Practice the "mental tapes" you made during your TV coding session.

CHECKLIST   *time spent*

☐ HAND-EYE COORDINATION EXERCISES   _____
☐ INTERMEDIATE SYBERRELAXATION
    EXERCISE   _____
☐ BASIC SYBER-CONCENTRATION
    EXERCISE   _____
☐ COLOR RECALL EXERCISE   _____
☐ PRACTICE TV MENTAL TAPES

DAY SEVENTEEN

1. Spend 15-30 minutes working at the Hand-Eye Coordination Exercises. (Optional)

2. If you are cross-dominant, work with your eye patch for an hour or two. (Optional)

3. Instead of the INTERMEDIATE SYBER-RELAXATION EXERCISE do the full BASIC program (remember, you do the full program one day a week). Do this twice today, followed by SYBER-CONCENTRATION (below).

4. Immediately following the Basic Syber-Relaxation Exercise

complete the BASIC SYBER-CONCENTRATION EXER-
CISE; simply tag it onto the end.

5. Practice the "mental tapes" you made during your TV
coding session.

CHECKLIST   *time spent*

☐ HAND-EYE COORDINATION EXERCISES   _____
☐ BASIC SYBERRELAXATION EXERCISE   _____
☐ BASIC SYBER-CONCENTRATION
    EXERCISE   _____
☐ PRACTICE TV MENTAL TAPES   _____

DAY EIGHTEEN

1. Spend 15-30 minutes working at the Hand-Eye Coordination
Exercises. (Optional)

2. If you are cross-dominant, work with your eye patch for an
hour or two. (Optional)

3. Complete INTERMEDIATE SYBER - RELAXATION
EXERCISE—do this twice daily followed by SYBER-
CONCENTRATION (below).

4. Immediately following the Intermediate Syber-Relaxation
Exercise complete the BASIC SYBER-CONCENTRATION
EXERCISE; simply tag it onto the end.

5. Practice the "mental tapes" you made during the TV coding session.

CHECKLIST   *time spent*

☐ HAND-EYE COORDINATION EXERCISES   _____
☐ INTERMEDIATE SYBERRELAXATION
   EXERCISE   _____
☐ BASIC SYBER-CONCENTRATION
   EXERCISE   _____
☐ PRACTICE TV MENTAL TAPES   _____

DAY NINETEEN

1. Spend 15-30 minutes working at the Hand-Eye Coordination Exercises. (Optional)

2. If you are cross-dominant, work with your eye patch for an hour or two. (Optional)

3. Complete INTERMEDIATE SYBER-RELAXATION EXERCISE—do this twice daily followed by SYBER-CONCENTRATION (below).

4. Immediately following the Intermediate Syber-Relaxation Exercise complete the BASIC SYBER-CONCENTRATION EXERCISE; simply tag it onto the end.

5. This could be game day. After you have played, try Recency Coding (see chapter 11). Remember, ideally, Recency Coding should be performed within six hours of play.

CHECKLIST   *time spent*

☐ HAND-EYE COORDINATION EXERCISES   _____
☐ INTERMEDIATE SYBERRELAXATION   _____
☐ BASIC SYBER-CONCENTRATION   _____
☐ RECENCY CODING   _____

DAY TWENTY

1. Spend 15-30 minutes working at the Hand-Eye Coordination Exercises. (Optional)

2. If you are cross-dominant, work with your eye patch for an hour or two. (Optional)

3. Complete INTERMEDIATE SYBER-RELAXATION EXERCISE—do this twice daily followed by SYBER-CONCENTRATION (below).

4. Immediately following the Intermediate Syber-Relaxation Exercise complete the BASIC SYBER-CONCENTRATION EXERCISE; simply tag it onto the end.

5. Input from television or from instruction (see chapter seven).

CHECKLIST   *time spent*

☐ HAND-EYE COORDINATION EXERCISES   _____
☐ INTERMEDIATE SYBERRELAXATION
   EXERCISE   _____

☐ BASIC SYBER-CONCENTRATION
    EXERCISE   _____
☐ PRACTICE TV MENTAL TAPES   _____

DAY TWENTY-ONE

1. Spend 15-30 minutes working at the Hand-Eye Coordination Exercises. (Optional)

2. If you are cross-dominant, work with your eye patch for an hour or two. (Optional)

3. As a refresher, spend 10 minutes studying and practicing eye-shift patterns.

4. Complete INTERMEDIATE SYBER-RELAXATION EXERCISE—do this twice daily followed by SYBER-CONCENTRATION (below).

5. Immediately following the Intermediate Syber-Relaxation Exercise complete the BASIC SYBER-CONCENTRATION EXERCISE; simply tag it onto the end.

6. Spend a few minutes practicing the Color Recall Exercise (six colors).

7. Practice the "mental tapes" you made during your TV coding session.

CHECKLIST   *time spent*

☐ HAND-EYE COORDINATION EXERCISES   _____

☐ STUDY EYE SHIFT CHART   _____
☐ INTERMEDIATE SYBERRELAXATION
  EXERCISE   _____
☐ BASIC SYBER-CONCENTRATION
  EXERCISE   _____
☐ COLOR RECALL EXERCISE   _____
☐ PRACTICE TV MENTAL TAPES   _____

DAY TWENTY-TWO

1. Spend 15-30 minutes working at the Hand-Eye Coordination Exercises. (Optional)

2. If you are cross-dominant, work with your eye patch for an hour or two. (Optional)

3. Complete INTERMEDIATE SYBER-RELAXATION EXERCISE—do this twice daily followed by SYBER-CONCENTRATION (below).

4. Immediately following the Intermediate Syber-Relaxation Exercise complete the BASIC SYBER-CONCENTRATION EXERCISE; simply tag it onto the end.

5. Spend a few minutes practicing the Color Recall Exercise (six colors).

6. Practice the "mental tapes" you made during your TV coding session.

CHECKLIST   *time spent*

☐ HAND-EYE COORDINATION EXERCISES   _____

☐ STUDY EYE SHIFT CHART _____
☐ INTERMEDIATE SYBERRELAXATION
   EXERCISE _____
☐ BASIC SYBER-CONCENTRATION
   EXERCISE _____
☐ COLOR RECALL EXERCISE _____
☐ PRACTICE TV MENTAL TAPES _____

DAY TWENTY-THREE

1. Spend 15-30 minutes working at the Hand-Eye Coordination Exercises. (Optional)

2. If you are cross-dominant, work with your eye patch for an hour or two. (Optional)

3. Complete INTERMEDIATE SYBER-RELAXATION EXERCISE—do this twice daily followed by SYBER-CONCENTRATION (below).

4. Immediately following the Intermediate Syber-Relaxation Exercise complete the BASIC SYBER-CONCENTRATION EXERCISE; simply tag it onto the end.

5. Spend a few minutes practicing the Color Recall Exercise (six colors).

6. Practice the "mental tapes" you made during your TV coding session.

CHECKLIST   *time spent*

- ☐ HAND-EYE COORDINATION EXERCISES   _____
- ☐ INTERMEDIATE SYBERRELAXATION
  EXERCISE   _____
- ☐ BASIC SYBER-CONCENTRATION
  EXERCISE   _____
- ☐ COLOR RECALL EXERCISE   _____
- ☐ PRACTICE TV MENTAL TAPES   _____

DAY TWENTY-FOUR

1. Spend 15-30 minutes working at the Hand-Eye Coordination Exercises. (Optional)

2. If you are cross-dominant, work with your eye patch for an hour or two. (Optional)

. Instead of the INTERMEDIATE SYBER-RELAXATION ERCISE do the full BASIC program. Do this twice today llowed by SYBER-CONCENTRATION (below).

4. Immediately following the BASIC Syber-Relaxation Exercise complete the BASIC SYBER-CONCENTRATION EXERCISE; simply tag it onto the end.

5. Spend a few minutes practicing the Color Recall Exercise (six colors).

6. Practice the "mental tapes" you made during your TV coding session.

CHECKLIST   *time spent*

☐ HAND-EYE COORDINATION EXERCISES   _____
☐ BASIC SYBERRELAXATION EXERCISE   _____
☐ BASIC SYBER-CONCENTRATION
  EXERCISE   _____
☐ COLOR RECALL EXERCISE   _____
☐ PRACTICE TV MENTAL TAPES   _____

DAY TWENTY-FIVE

1. Spend 15-30 minutes working at the Hand-Eye Coordination Exercises. (Optional)

2. If you are cross-dominant, work with your eye patch for an hour or two. (Optional)

3. Complete INTERMEDIATE SYBER-RELAXATION EXERCISE—do this twice daily followed by SYBER-CONCENTRATION (below).

4. Immediately following the Intermediate Syber-Relaxation Exercise complete the BASIC SYBER-CONCENTRATION EXERCISE; simply tag it onto the end.

5. Spend a few minutes practicing the Color Recall Exercise (six colors).

6. PREGAME REHEARSAL.

CHECKLIST   *time spent*

☐ HAND-EYE COORDINATION EXERCISES   _____
☐ INTERMEDIATE SYBERRELAXATION
    EXERCISE   _____
☐ BASIC SYBER-CONCENTRATION
    EXERCISE   _____
☐ COLOR RECALL EXERCISE
☐ PREGAME REHEARSAL

DAY TWENTY-SIX

1. Spend 15-30 minutes working at the Hand-Eye Coordination Exercises. (Optional)

2. If you are cross-dominant, work with your eye patch for an hour or two. (Optional)

3. Complete INTERMEDIATE SYBER-RELAXATION EXERCISE—do this twice daily followed by SYBER-CONCENTRATION (below).

4. Immediately following the Intermediate Syber-Relaxation Exercise complete the BASIC SYBER-CONCENTRATION EXERCISE; simply tag it onto the end.

5. This could be a game day. After you have played, try Recency Coding (see chapter 11). Remember, ideally, Recency Coding should be performed within six hours of play.

CHECKLIST   *time spent*

☐ HAND-EYE COORDINATION EXERCISES   _____
☐ INTERMEDIATE SYBERRELAXATION
    EXERCISE   _____
☐ BASIC SYBER-CONCENTRATION
    EXERCISE   _____
☐ RECENCY CODING   _____

DAY TWENTY-SEVEN

1. Spend 15-30 minutes working at the Hand-Eye Coordination Exercises. (Optional)

2. If you are cross-dominant, work with your eye patch for an hour or two. (Optional)

3. Complete INTERMEDIATE SYBER-RELAXATION EXERCISE—do this twice daily followed by SYBER-CONCENTRATION (below).

4. Immediately following the Intermediate Syber-Relaxation Exercise complete the BASIC SYBER-CONCENTRATION EXERCISE; simply tag it onto the end.

5. Input from television or from instruction (see chapter seven).

CHECKLIST   *time spent*

☐ HAND-EYE COORDINATION EXERCISES   _____
☐ INTERMEDIATE SYBERRELAXATION
    EXERCISE   _____

☐ BASIC SYBER-CONCENTRATION
    EXERCISE   _____
☐ PRACTICE TV MENTAL TAPES   _____

DAY TWENTY-EIGHT

1. Spend 15-30 minutes working at the Hand-Eye Coordination Exercises. (Optional)

2. If you are cross-dominant, work with your eye patch for an hour or two. (Optional)

3. As a refresher, spend 10 minutes studying and practicing eye-shift patterns.

4. Complete INTERMEDIATE SYBER-RELAXATION EXERCISE—do this twice daily followed by SYBER-CONCENTRATION (below).

    Immediately following the Intermediate Syber-Relaxation ercise complete the BASIC SYBER-CONCENTRATION XERCISE; simply tag it onto the end.

6. Spend a few minutes practicing the Color Recall Exercise (six colors).

7. Practice the "mental tapes" you made during your TV coding session.

CHECKLIST   *time spent*

☐ HAND-EYE COORDINATION EXERCISES   _____

☐ STUDY EYE SHIFT CHART   _____
☐ INTERMEDIATE SYBERRELAXATION
   EXERCISES   _____
☐ BASIC SYBER-CONCENTRATION
   EXERCISE   _____
☐ COLOR RECALL EXERCISE   _____
☐ PRACTICE TV MENTAL TAPES   _____

DAY TWENTY-NINE

1. Spend 15-30 minutes working at the Hand-Eye Coordination Exercises. (Optional)

2. If you are cross-dominant, work with your eye patch for an hour or two. (Optional)

3. Complete INTERMEDIATE SYBER-RELAXATION EXERCISE—do this twice daily followed by SYBER CONCENTRATION (below).

4. Immediately following the Intermediate Syber-Relaxation Exercise complete the BASIC SYBER-CONCENTRATION EXERCISE; simply tag it onto the end.

5. Spend a few minutes practicing the Color Recall Exercise (six colors).

6. Practice the "mental tapes" you made during your TV coding session.

CHECKLIST   *time spent*

☐ HAND-EYE COORDINATION EXERCISES   _____
☐ INTERMEDIATE SYBERRELAXATION
     EXERCISE   _____
☐ BASIC SYBER-CONCENTRATION
     EXERCISE   _____
☐ COLOR RECALL EXERCISE   _____
☐ PRACTICE TV MENTAL TAPES   _____

DAY THIRTY

1. Spend 15-30 minutes working at the Hand-Eye Coordination Exercises. (Optional)

2. If you are cross-dominant, work with your eye patch for an hour or two. (Optional)

   Complete INTERMEDIATE SYBER-RELAXATION ERCISE—do this twice daily followed by SYBER-CONCENTRATION (below).

4. Immediately following the Intermediate Syber-Relaxation Exercise complete the BASIC SYBER-CONCENTRATION EXERCISE; simply tag it onto the end.

5. Spend a few minutes practicing the Color Recall Exercise (six colors).

6. Practice the "mental tapes" you made during your TV coding session.

CHECKLIST   *time spent*

☐ HAND-EYE COORDINATION EXERCISES   _____
☐ INTERMEDIATE SYBERRELAXATION
  EXERCISE   _____
☐ BASIC SYBER-CONCENTRATION
  EXERCISE   _____
☐ COLOR RECALL EXERCISE   _____
☐ PRACTICE TV MENTAL TAPES   _____

NOTE: After six-to-eight weeks, relaxation/oxygenation and sharp concentration should become a conditioned reflex that you are able to summon at will. At this point, you simply cue into the activating color with an upper left eye shift, progressing from RED through VIOLET for each of the six Syber Zones. In other words, your *total exercise* for relaxation and concentration is as follows:

1. Upper left ESC. Cue into the activating color RED.
2. Repeat for the color ORANGE.
3. Repeat for the color YELLOW.
4. Repeat for the color GREEN.
5. Repeat for the color BLUE.
6. Repeat for the color VIOLET.

14

Sample SyberVision Training Schedule

After you have conditioned all of the necessary responses and mastered all of the SyberVision techniques and discipline (this will take approximately 30 days), you will be able to put yourself on a regular training schedule. Suppose you have a game or a match scheduled on a Saturday, here's how your weekly SyberVision schedule would work:

SUNDAY
Code televised sports programming following procedures outlined in Chapter 6.

MONDAY
Put yourself through the full Syber-Relaxation/Oxygenation Conditioning discipline with tensing and breathing, extending into the Syber-Concentration Conditioning to the Violet/ Corpus Callosum area of the brain. Chapters 4 and 5.

TUESDAY
Recency coding from television, lessons, practice or previous competition. Chapter 11.

WEDNESDAY
Recency coding from television, lessons, practice or previous competition. Chapter 11.

THURSDAY
"Syber-Demon"—"Syber-Man," "Syber-Woman" conditioning. Chapter 9.

FRIDAY
No sooner than 24 hours before competition, put yourself though a full session of "SyberVision Pre-Competition Performance Coding". If your competition extends over one day or if you compete on a more frequent basis than once per week, use this time to code up to a week's worth of performance. Chapter 8.

SATURDAY
Play pre-selected music prior to competition. Assess your confidence/anxiety level prior to competition, utilizing the "Syber-Demon" — "Syber-Man" conditioning technique. Activate SyberVision encoded memory by Upper Left ESC/ Violet. After competition, go through post-competition/ recency coding. Chapter 9.